The Maryland colonists prepare to erect St. Clement's Island cross. (EPFL)

MARYLAND
A Picture History • 1632-1976

The arms of the Calverts, barons of Baltimore and founders of Maryland. Rendered in stone, the crests were used as line markers in the survey of the Mason-Dixon line, alternating with the crest of the Penns of Pennsylvania. (MHS)

MARYLAND

A Picture History • 1632-1976

Commentary by Carleton Jones

PUBLISHED BY BODINE & ASSOCIATES, INC. BALTIMORE, MARYLAND • 1976

The first Marylanders, the Susquehannock Indians, from an old German map of the period. (MHS)

First Edition
Copyright 1976
Bodine & Associates, Inc.
Library of Congress
Catalog No. 75-36657
Standard Book No.
910254-09-5
Printed in U.S.A.

PREFACE

I AM FREQUENTLY ASKED which book on Maryland history is best for general reading. Much depends on the type of person making the request. For the scholar there was really only one book which covered the whole state: Matthew P. Andrews' *History of Maryland* (1929). His *Tercentenary History of Maryland* in four volumes does not compare because it is mainly biographical. But the history has serious faults; the coverage of colonial history is good but the later years are weak, and of course by now it is almost half a century out of date. To remedy this deficiency a team of scholars under the editorship of Walsh and Fox produced *Maryland: A History, 1632-1974*. It was funded by the State of Maryland, and it completely superseded Andrews. This, then, is the history for scholars.

But most people wanting to learn about Maryland want to do it without struggle and hardship. Not for them the laborious study chapter by chapter but rather a book which can be picked up at odd moments, a book which can be checked for a date or for a pithy study of the causes of the War of 1812. *My Maryland* by Kaessmann, Manakee and Wheeler is by far the best book for any adult wanting to learn the easy way, and it has become the textbook for schools throughout America. All three authors knew just what schoolchildren wanted, and I doubt it was accidental that it was also to become perfect for adults, particularly useful for those who are from out of state and want to know quickly the salient points in Maryland history. It is likely to remain a must for all but the scholar.

One little book, not too well known, is authored by a Baltimorean, Edgar Heyl, *I Didn't Know That!* This settles arguments on first happenings in Maryland and is therefore in itself a form of history for Maryland.

Maryland has several good illustrations, and *My Maryland* has hundreds, including portraits. But there has long been a need for a picture book of Maryland, in which a tremendous variety of illustrations, all of top class, could be assembled in a handsomely designed book. Simply to show good pictures would not suffice, of course, and I have read with great interest and admiration Carelton Jones' *Maryland: A Picture History*. Each illustration has solid facts accompanying it, with a short, succinct narrative which will give the reader all he needs to know unless a paper or study is needed, when the abovementioned books should be consulted. All manner of facts, scarcely known by the Marylander, are given, and many of the illustrations are reproduced for the first time. The choice will no doubt startle some readers when they see how many are held by the Enoch Pratt Free Library, the Maryland Historical Society, and the Peale Museum.

The narrative is rapid and succinct, and it is written especially for readers who do not have the time or the need to study the weightier tomes. Having read the whole book and having seen the felicitous use of the illustrations, I can feel certain that this book should be welcomed in every Maryland home.

On a personal note, I can look at Maryland as an immigrant; I came here in 1957, and after visiting almost every other state in the Union I find that Maryland is foremost in my affection; it seems to like Britishers more than any other state!

P. W. Filby
Director
Maryland Historical Society,
Baltimore

The arms of Charles I, King of Scotland, Ireland and England (EPFL)

FOREWORD

IN 1632, FOR A SHARE of all the gold and silver found, plus two arrowheads a year, King Charles I granted the colony of Maryland to George Calvert, Lord Baltimore. If this seems like a remote event, there is no reason to feel strange about it. We are as far in time from the founders of Maryland as they were from the end of the Crusades in the Holy Land.

That long range of time—344 years—has swept away all but the most remote physical vestiges of Seventeenth Century Maryland and scarcely anything but artifacts, a fort or manor house or two, remains more or less unchanged for us today.

This book is a graphic attempt to show how it changed and to give some dimension to the Maryland legend. Romantic novels of the past and movies of more recent vintage have tended to distort the state's image. It was a place of broadly rolling plantations and rich horse farms where portraits of Cavaliers hung on the walls. Behind each pillared portico lurked a southern belle, repulsing, or in some cases, not repulsing, the advances of the Yankee cavalrymen.

Every true Marylander, said a corollary of the tale, leaped on his horse with spurs jangling to save the Southern Confederacy or spied on the "invaders" if the resident was a hoop-skirted female.

The truth is vastly larger and quite different. Maryland was a significant force in the colonization of the western south. It was the first southern state to develop a full range of mercantile economy before the Civil War. It was an arsenal of victory in the Civil War.

It housed, as it houses today, the oldest large urban black population in the country, as well as one of the most diversified foreign populations in America.

An odd thing is that the state has always resisted superlatives and has almost universally chosen the moderate, even the modest course. It has had fun doing it, as some of these illustrations reveal.

Modern historians have noted that while New Englanders spent their time writing books, Colonial Virginians read books, mostly Latin and the classics, while the Annapolitans and the wealth of Maryland colony caught up on the latest London gossip and went to the theater.

That sort of mood made Baltimore and the spas of the Chesapeake the golden resort of Southern wealth before the Civil War as well as the playground of the New York plutocracy later on during the Gilded Age.

Today, wedded to the fate of the billion windowed millions of Bosh-Wash, the eastern super city, Maryland has to fight to retain remaining historic, cultural and natural resources, in many cases still untouched and carefully tended by private and public care.

Maryland was an important Colonial experiment that built a public sense of freedom out of what was probably the most private of all the 13 original colonies. Its Bay was the supermarket and the beltway of the Eighteenth Century middle Atlantic, a key to developing the sort of enriched economy that could survive both revolution and civil war.

It could not have done this without its people, its spirit and in no small degree the artists and photographers who made this record possible.

The Ark *and the* Dove, *vessels of Maryland's future.* (PE)

CONTENTS

The Tidewater Barony	9
Thrust Toward Freedom	15
The Slender Link	26
Gold and Glory	35
Lavender and Lamplight	54
The Forgotten Arsenal	74
The Bannered Years	100
Progress and Poverty	128
War and Peace	150

1634 — 1690
THE TIDEWATER BARONY

INTRODUCTION

In MARCH OF 1634, a small party of about 20 "gentlemen" and 200 servants and adventurers landed with awe and thanks on St. Clement's Island in the lower stretches of the north bank of the Potomac.

Most, accustomed to England's tiny scale, could not believe there was any river in the world that size. They prayed, erected a cross and soon selected a permanent site for settlement about 30 miles to the east off the St. Mary's river.

On board with the *Ark* and the *Dove* party, sailing with what were respectively a 160-ton ship and a tiny pinnace of about 50 tons, was Leonard Calvert. Charles Stuart had created the Maryland colony for Leonard's uncle, George Calvert, first baron Baltimore, but his lordship, a veteran explorer and wealthy Yorkshireman, died before he could venture west. Cecil (Cecilius), who became second lord, stayed home to run things.

The colonists found abundant fish and game that spring and Piscataway Indians who seemed to be friendly. But there were rumors of more fierce Susquehannocks not far away.

A water mill seems to have been on the agenda. Soon the colonists discovered they had a rival for their land other than the Indians. William Claiborne, a contentious Virginia adventurer had taken up a settlement a few years before on Kent Island, part of Lord Baltimore's grant, and couldn't be budged, a seed of later trouble.

The Calverts had virtually royal powers in Maryland, but tended to rule with a velvet glove. They were thoroughly scared by the first turbulent 25 years of the Virginia company. By 1635 an assembly of the colony was meeting and soon, rather surprisingly, claiming the right to initiate legislation on its own.

There was relative quiet. The colony, by an accident of geography, was screened by an impenetrable, closely packed thicket that covered much of north central Maryland and was similar to Virginia's wilderness country, without the swamps.

Traditionally, the southern Maryland necks and eddies were hunting grounds, rather than homes, for the great tribes to the north and south of tiny St. Mary's settlement. It is hard to believe, but tradition has it that one Patuxent chief bent over backwards to make the colonists feel at home.

"I love the English so well, that if they should go about to kill me, I would command the people not to revenge my death; for I know they would not do such a thing, except it were through my own fault," said the chief to a conference between Leonard Calvert and Sir John Harvey, the Virginia governor.

Nothing could protect the colony, however, from the waves of Constitutional and religious turmoil that struck England in the Seventeenth Century. The execution of Charles I in 1649, the restoration of Charles II in 1660 and the elimination of James II in 1688 all had ferocious impact on Colonial destinies.

There was a see-sawing of control in Maryland province, usually between pro and anti-Puritan elements and it is wholly wrong to think of the colony as a peaceful entity, prospering at tidewater while the rest of the world brawled.

There was a continuous, almost circular movement of people in and around the colony, especially in later years of the Colonial period. It was driven on by local famines, lowland fevers, land grabs and land sales.

Puritans fled the wrath of Stuart agents in Virginia and came to Maryland colony. Marylanders moved on to settle western North Carolina. The Tuscaroras fled North Carolina, crossing the state for refuge in New York. German-born Pennsylvanians moved into Western Maryland and Huguenots and Acadians entered the colony after the French defeats in Canada.

The closeness to England never left, however, and it never failed to have usually negative impact. Maryland was, if not the engine, at least the pathway of middle Atlantic turmoil. That is the beginning of its political story.

The favor of 6.7 million acres

The roots of Maryland colony are favors granted by King James I, beginning in 1617 to the wealthy Yorkshire family in England named Calvert.

Tragic King Charles I continued the tradition, granting to George Calvert, first Lord Baltimore, the province of Maryland shortly before his death. A few months later the charter of Maryland was made official in the name of Calvert's son, Cecil, second baron of Baltimore.

Though decidedly forward looking for its day, and styled to profit by earlier disasters in colonization, there is more than a hint in the charter, which Charles I helped write, of the only-good-Indian-is-a-dead Indian attitude, later to plague the United States.

King Charles and his agents wrote that the settlers could pursue the Indians "even beyond the limits of their province," remembering the massacres of the 1620's in Virginia. The document hit the Indians as savages "having no knowledge of the Divine Being." It gave colonists the right to kill, or to spare, Indian captives as they chose.

Founding the colony

Sailing from England in November of 1633, Cecil Calvert's costly venture (it cost 40,000 pounds) arrived on Maryland shores on March 25 of the next year after a short stop in the West Indies.

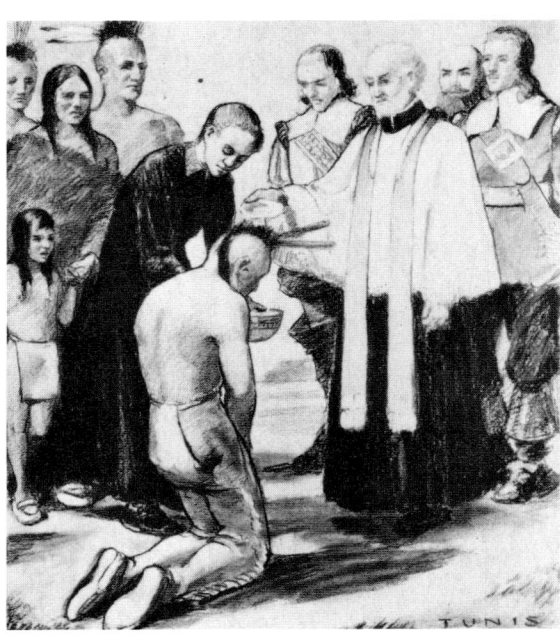

The Piscataway chief, Kittamagund, is baptized by Father Andrew White in a symbolic ceremony of 1639. From a drawing by Edwin Tunis. (EPFL)

Generally peaceful relations with the Indians kept Maryland from repeating scenes like this one from the early days on the Colonial frontier. (LC)

The colonists planted a cross on St. Clement's Island and began the arduous business of settlement, putting down crops to stave off the starvation that had been the bane of the two previous English ventures in Massachusetts and Virginia.

From the first, the group was mixed in religion and race. The *Ark* and the *Dove* carried two black migrants, Mathias Sousa and John Mimus and possibly a third. Catholics were in the minority and had been cautioned by the Calverts to keep a low profile in this age of intolerance.

They agreed, however, on the necessity of faith and soon were working to convert the "savages." Leonard Calvert proved an excellent administrator. He needed to be.

The task of settlement, cabin-building and land clearance, a diorama at the Maryland Historical Society. (MHS)

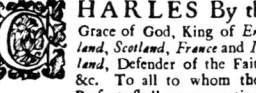

The Maryland charter of 1632. It was remarkable in its day for its detailed directions on how to proceed. (EPFL)

King Charles I, royal grantor of the Maryland charter. An angry parliament beheaded him in 1649. (LC)

George Calvert, first Lord Baltimore, never saw the Maryland he was given, but he founded a chilly Canadian colony, Avalon and was roughly treated on a trip to Virginia because of his conversion to Catholicism. (EPFL)

The St. Mary's colonial capitol restoration, based on drawings of the 1670's. (AAB)

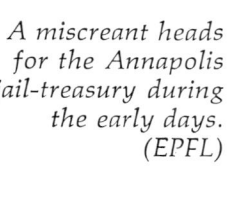

A miscreant heads for the Annapolis jail-treasury during the early days. (EPFL)

Cross Manor, home of the influential Cornwalleys family, oldest brick house in Maryland. (AAB)

Life in the early days

It was the idea of the Calverts to create manorial estates in Maryland, large holdings similar to those in the English shires.

Though planting began early, and was a success almost wholly because of tobacco, it didn't work out that way. Small farms of 250 acres or so undercut the ambitions of creating a new world aristocracy.

A vocal assembly, active as early as 1635, was coping with upstart William Claiborne, of Kent Island, who asserted his claims of precedence over the Calverts, on the grounds of earlier settlement.

For most of the colonists, the immediate future was the arduous one of clearing the land.

Settings for cavaliers and puritans

The slow physical development of Maryland colony did not mask the fact that it was making money for its sponsors. By the 1660's, tobacco duties from Maryland and neighboring Virginia were producing 25 per cent of England's customs revenue. Luxuries were, however slow to come back across the Atlantic the other way.

Shipbuilding got underway on the Miles and Chester rivers within a decade of the founding of the colony and things were prosperous enough for the first horse race, which was held in Talbot county in 1672.

Colonial law continued to emphasize iron-clad male chauvinism. In the 1650's, an officer of the colony, Capt. William Mitchell was fined 5,000 pounds of tobacco for adultery. The woman involved was sentenced to 39 lashes.

Mistress Margaret Brent, a Calvert connection, had a more independent attitude, and in 1648 appear before the general assembly, demanding a vote.

The great English upheaval which brought in Oliver Cromwell as Lord Protector brought thousands of Puritans to Maryland colony, fleeing the wrath of Virginia. They founded the Annapolis district. A generation after the landing, Maryland population was only about 10,000, but included one of the most homogenous religious communities in north America, a mixture of Catholics, Quakers, Presbyterians, Anabaptists and a sprinkling of Anglicans. The first Jewish immigrant, Jacob Lumbrozo, of Lisbon, arrived in 1656.

A possible magnet was the colony's famous Acts of Toleration of 1649, passed by the assembly in a day when religion was always political.

It said that no person professing belief in Jesus Christ could be punished for his religion or prevented from expressing it in the province. Belief in God was essential to citizenship, however; blasphemy carried the death penalty.

There were other dangers. Some historians report that Rebecca Fowler was executed in 1685 in Calvert county for "witchcraft, enchantments, charms and sorceries."

Two protagonists, separated by an ocean

These men typified two strains in English colonial life—loyalty to the crown and executive power versus freebooting adventure.

Autocratic Cecilius Calvert always landed on his feet during the execution-prone seventeenth century and he takes rank as one of Britain's greatest colonial administrators. He ruled Maryland for 42 years with something of a sense of humor. If there was any poverty in the colony, said his lordship, it came from "brandewine and other liquors." (EPFL)

William Claiborne, baron of Kent Island, was ready to pounce on the colony and the proprietorship for 25 years and he had important allies in London. He fought a naval engagement in the Pocomoke river battling the forces from St. Mary's, returned 20 years later to seize the colony during the Puritan interregnum in England. (VSL)

Leonard Calvert treats with the Indians. Cloth and axes changed hands in return for 30 miles of Potomac river frontage. (EPFL)

"The miracle of this age"

Victorian historians censored him for his salty language, but a lively Londoner, born in 1638, who came to Maryland when he was about 20 has left us one of the best word pictures of the colony.

He was George Alsop, perhaps the first person to hint that Maryland was "fun." He says seafood in the colony was "catched with very much ease" to the "great refreshment of the inhabitants of the province."

Local Indians, he reports, were buried in full battle dress in the seated position. He praises the St. Mary's settlement for having rid itself of "all inquisitions, martyrdom and banishments."

There were wild deer and wild hogs all over the place by the 1660's, plus a quiet and "sober government." Anyone who wanted peace, said the state's first chamber of commerce spokesman should "look on Maryland with eyes admiring, and he'le then judge her The Miracle of this Age."

Signifying the takeover of the colony by the king in 1692 was the "Great Seal Deputed of Maryland." It was used for writs and other documents. The original weighed 38 ounces in silver. (MHS)

The peppery poet and commentator, Alsop, drew this "landskip" of Maryland province and worked in a beaver hunt. North is to your right. (EPFL)

1690 — 1776
THRUST TOWARD FREEDOM

IN DECEMBER OF 1688, James II, last Catholic king of England, was allowed to escape to France to the infinite relief of almost everybody. This far-off act was to have earth-shaking consequences in Maryland. The incoming Protestant power lost no time in making changes. By 1692, the province had been converted officially into a crown colony like neighboring Virginia and the Calvert proprietorship shoved aside, though the family continued to enjoy its five-figure annual income. The changeover brought reaction. The pioneering Acts of Toleration were negated and the Anglican church was established as a burden on the taxpayer. Harsh acts of disability against Catholics banned public worship.

The royal reign continued for a generation and by the time the Calverts, converted to Protestantism, returned in 1715 they found a much-changed principality.

Slavery had spread and the new ports, including Port Tobacco and Annapolis, now the colonial capital, moved bodily to the Providence district of Anne Arundel from St. Mary's city by autocratic Sir Francis Nicholson, were beginning to thrive.

Port life, and the need for tradespeople of all kinds began to differentiate Maryland from Virginia, though collectively both provinces were more important to England financially than all the rest of the colonies put together.

In Virginia, it was royal policy to foster great tidewater estates, especially in the wealthy Northern Neck district.

The Calvert proprietorship had already found out that this would not work in Maryland. Consequently there were few counterparts in the colony of the semi-royal establishments to the south, other than the Ridgelys of Hampton, the Dorseys of Belmont, the Lloyds of Wye and the Carrolls. In Eighteenth Century Maryland, the county courts assumed important, widespread functions that pretty much governed the people day by day. It was the general assembly, however, that gave people fits in England. In 1731, Governor Samuel Ogle complained to Charles Calvert that Maryland was showing "strange and unreasonable jealousies and prejudices against your lordship's government."

For 50 years before the Revolution, Maryland assemblymen never ceased to raise vigorous hell, demanding the right to control their own meetings, handle the purse strings and they went so far as to freeze out pro-Calvert

Strangest sight in Maryland during the Eighteenth Century was the Baltimore court house, built in 1768 and later fitted with masonry stilts when a hill was cut down to take Calvert street northward. (PM)

and crown appointees from their membership. Colonial governors had at once more, and less, power than the king back home. They could override acts of the assembly, something the English crown had to give up as early as 1707.

The governors, however, could not build a political power base. In the end it proved fatal. They could not manipulate the assembly, or the money, something English rulers could do for two generations after the American Revolution.

In 1774, the distinguished English commentator, William Eddis wrote from Maryland that "All America is in flames! I hear strange language every day." So it was, and so it was to be.

Days of glory on the tidewater

Early in the 1700s, Annapolis and a few other sheltered Bay ports began to take shape as winter resorts for refugees from chilly tobacco and wheat farms. George Washington, later in the century, would repeat the pattern, loping over to Annapolis and tidewater country for the races after a stopover with friends on the Calvert county side of the Potomac. Benjamin Franklin took his leisure in the region, playing his famous musical glasses for a festive gathering.

Not all the portraits that floated back to England about the colony were flattering in the early days, however. Ebenezer Cook, a minor

A symbol of the vivacious Annapolis social life, the Tuesday Club, passing the pipe. At another Annapolis club, the penalty for boisterous conduct was drinking a glass of water and keeping quiet—for one minute. (MHS)

Masthead of The Maryland Gazette, founded in 1729 and later an influential organ of revolutionary doings. (MHS)

Tobacco, transhipped to Europe via England, was the basis for most of the new-found Colonial wealth. (AAB

English poet, painted Maryland as a ramshackle, rude settlement, filled with cutpurses and swindlers in his "The Sot Weed Factor." of 1708.

In Annapolis, the general assembly was a partial magnet from the 1690's on, but so were the comforts and amenities of the town later. The huge urban mansions that are the glory of Annapolis and are amazing survivals reflect this life. They were built not because their owners were pretentious or had 15 children, but because their owners' *circles* were large. The social crowds, friends and relatives had to be spared nights in the execrable Colonial inns where guests slept three or four to a bed and the food could only be imagined.

A prohibition law governing the colony was universally ignored. Annapolis was the scene of more than one ball where several hundred bottles of wine, brandy and sack were consumed by only several hundred guests.

Annapolitans were great readers and theatergoers, wearers of the latest London fashions and they joyed in topical novels and the serious poetry of the Augustan age. Portrait painters, cabinet makers and silversmiths flocked to the capital to service the new elegance in a town that travelers said over and over again was "more English" than any other place in America.

A newspaper began in 1729 and horse-breeding of thoroughbred quality about 1745.

It did not please everybody. Trumpet-voiced George Whitefield, (1714-1770), revivalist orator and foe of sin and satin took one look at Maryland society in the 1740's and sniffed that the colony's women were "as much enslaved to their fashionable diversions as men . . . to their bottle and their hounds."

The wealthy colony looked like this to a cartographer in 1757. (EPFL)

Charles Willson Peale, with palette at left, captured the pre-Revolutionary ambience of Annapolis and the colonial age when he painted this 1773 view of his family. Peggy Dugan, servant and nurse, folds her hands at right. (EPFL)

Chevroned brick work, with glazed headers, decorated the newly-opulent Maryland country homes. This is Fassit House, Worcester county. (EPFL)

Tidewater nursed many artists of high calibre, including Peale and the Peale family and John Shaw, supreme Annapolis cabinetmaker whose work is revered for the simple perfection of styling. None were more talented than William Buckland (1734-1774) an emigre who was also a master mason, carpenter and architect. His Hammond-Harwood house, the dining room of which experts regard as the most perfect Georgian room in America, and a score of other Maryland and Virginia buildings are at the top of the Colonial design heirarchy. Gunston Hall, White Hall on the Severn, Montpelier, Tulip Hill, the Chase-Lloyd house and the Brice House are among the master works.

Signs of the new opulence

Maryland men and women were traveling by mid-century, visiting others of the gentry, building mansions larger than any contemporary inns and even going to college in Europe, being painted there and taking the grand tour. Some symbols of that age:

Tulip Hill, the Galloway country estate in Anne Arundel. (AAB)

The garden front of the Hammond-Harwood house. (DS)

The Chase-Lloyd mansion, tallest of Buckland's triumphs. (AAB)

Montpelier, princely Snowden seat in Prince Georges county. (AAB)

Frank Mayer's rendering of a courtly tidewater visit. The sedan chair was favored for city travel. (EPFL)

Sir Joshua Reynolds, the English portraitist, catches willowy Mrs. Richard Lloyd of Maryland leaving a bit of vernal graffiti on the landscape. (EPFL)

Charles Carroll, the Barrister, influential focus for the new legal life that centered on the upper bay, built Mount Clare, sole surviving Colonial mansion in the Baltimore city limits. Martha Washington stopped there for a brief collation in the stormy Revolutionary days. (MHS)

Wealthy Edward Lloyd of Wye, called "The Patriot" (1744-1791), poses tranquilly with his lute-playing wife, but noisier days were ahead. Governor Lloyd opposed the royal fees, supported the Constitution. (EPFL)

Lordly Hampton, home of the slaveholding Ridgelys, near Towson. (AAB)

A slow start for Baltimore

Colonial surveyors in 1730 took a peaceful cove of the Patapsco and laid out a town chartered the year before, but it was a generation before their plotted center, first called Jones town, became a village.

Boston, Philadelphia and New York were already well-established Colonial ports when the survey of the 60-acre tract was begun. Squared off lots of about one acre were established with north and south diagonal streets prominent. But Baltimore was to grow mainly east and west.

An outpost in the west. Cumberland was the furthest travel outpost through the colonial period. A Nineteenth Century view. (EPFL)

Laying out Baltimore town, a Nineteenth Century version. (PM)

The new center in 1752 when it had "hardly 50 houses" according to one traveler. (EPFL)

Winners and losers in governing the west

Late in the seventeenth century, the Stuart family had shaved off a triangular patch of the Eastern shore to create Delaware, but the exact Pennsylvania boundaries remained in limbo.

In 1732, Charles Calvert, Fifth Lord Baltimore, came to America to straighten things out, but was forced to surrender a huge slice of what he thought was Maryland to the Penn family. It included about 4,000 square miles, 20 miles deep of part of the York-Lancaster corridor, some of the richest farm land in America. Daniel Dulany, the elder, fared better. He came to the colony as an indentured servant, dealt heavily in the western lands and became one of the wealthiest men in Maryland, and was sometimes called the nation's first land developer.

Horatio Sharpe, Colonial governor, finally straightened out the borderline by presiding over the final survey of the lands by Charles Mason and Jeremiah Dixon, English astronomers.

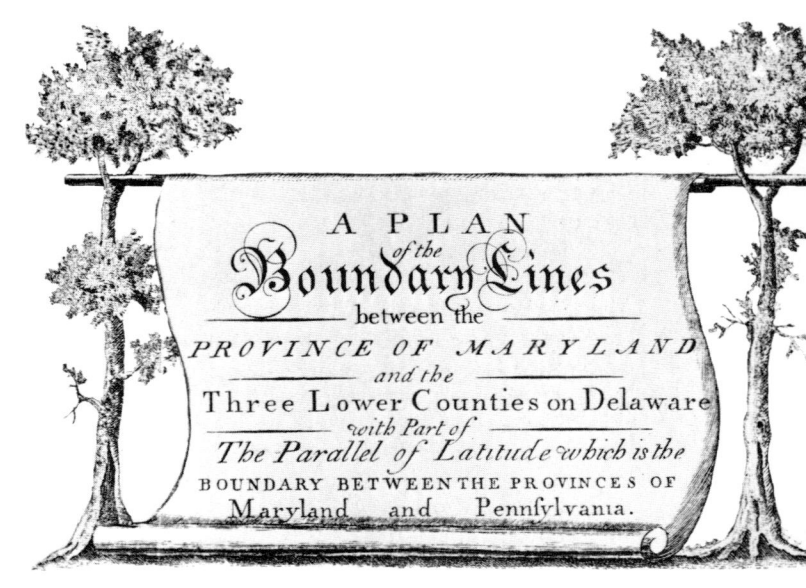

Title page of the printed survey by Mason and Dixon (BS)

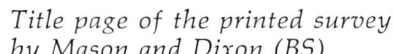

Daniel Dulany, the elder (MHS)

Gov. Horatio Sharpe (EPFL)

Charles Calvert, 5th Lord Baltimore (MHS)

Final acts of the drama

In 1692, the Maryland colony was a faraway province of perhaps 30,000 souls to be disposed of at the whim of a royal council in London. By 1774 it was a vigorous adolescent, ten times larger in population with the ability to act on its own.

It shared a spirit of dissent, unhappiness with the constant series of gouging acts which the British parliament had voted in order to bail themselves out of a debt of more than 100 million pounds, run up by the defense of Canada and the east coast of America.

The stamp act in the mid-1760's was the first major rumble of trouble. Since most printers were postmen and dealt in the legal field, the stamp act was a senseless inflammation of the very people in control of communications in the colonies and most likely to yell their heads off. Some acts and actors in the drama:

A postal service is organized by William Goddard, who advertises the opening of a "constitutional" and independent rival of crown services in 1774. (EPFL)

Baltimore's post office, a focal point in the gathering storm. (EPFL)

Annapolitans force the owner to burn the Peggy Stewart in protest against the tea tariff. (BS)

Shocks from the north and debates. . . .

Nothing hit Maryland people more than the arbitrary closing of the port of Boston by the British in 1774. With its growing emphasis on trade, the port empire on the Chesapeake began to see the handwriting on the wall.

The split in attitude between moderate elements and outright spokesmen for freedom received classic illustration in a debate between Charles Carroll of Carrollton and Daniel Dulany, the younger. Squaring off in 1773 in the *Maryland Gazette* under pseudonymns that everyone recognized, the two leaders of the colony debated the treatment of fees due the British crown. The restive read the debate throughout the colonies and hitherto peaceful gentry were converted overnight into hotheads, fearing the starvation that was to be visited on Massachusetts and its merchants and workers.

Charles Carroll of Carrollton. (EPFL)

Daniel Dulany the younger. (MHS)

A listening post during the crucial years, John Beale Bordley, (1727-1804), was high in the royal councils, made the transition to independence and as Maryland's most brilliant judge, was caught in this pose by Charles Willson Peale. (EPFL)

Changing the guard...

The sun set on the British empire in Maryland on June 23, 1776, when genial, socially-popular Sir Robert Eden, colonial governor, boarded the British warship *Fowey* and sailed away quietly. Maryland's life as an independent state began a few months later in February, 1777 when Thomas Johnson was elected the first governor.

Sir Robert Eden (EPFL)

Thomas Johnson (MHS)

1776 1783

THE SLENDER LINK

THE OUTBREAK OF THE REVOLUTION found Maryland in uncertain shape economically, no matter how united her leaders might have been politically.

A cycle of boom and bust in the tobacco trade was disheartening and, although the Annapolis and Baltimore wheat trade had grown phenominally since mid-century, the economy was tight, plagued with unemployment brought on by heavy immigration into the colony and the freeing of indentured servants.

There is little question that the Maryland economy, however, in relatively sheltered position, boomed during the conflict. Something like 225 Maryland privateering vessels received state and national letters of "marque and reprisal" for profitable sallies against the British merchant fleet. This may have been 20 per cent of all American raiders, fearless chance takers seeking plunder who seized seven British ships for every one lost. In numbers their crews far outnumbered the Continental Army.

On land, the state assembled the famous "Maryland Line", regulars of our first army, by and large the young, the unemployed and the venturesome. They traveled farther and usually hung around longer than almost any other state's forces in this war of seasonal dropouts and summer soldiers. Four outstanding men led them, a reminder that in Maryland, things usually go by fours, four signers of the Declaration, the Johns Hopkins "Big Four", etc.

There is a general impression among eastern historians that the Maryland assembly was less than generous to the nation and balked at making crucial sacrifices, especially financial at key points in the war.

As late as the winter of 1780-1781 Gen. Mordecai Gist and the great southern commander, Nathanael Greene, went begging before the Maryland board of war, with little result. The soldiery was different, they stayed with it from the defense of Boston through Yorktown.

Maryland was the essential, the slender link of communications between Williamsburg and Philadelphia, between the iron determination of New England to end it forever and the wild and bloody civil war that was the southern campaign.

State troops panicked more than once and on one occasion, the retreat through New Jersey in 1776, simply went home when their enlistments were up. On other fields, they turned the tide in three or four critical battles, facing, be it remembered, not amateurs but disciplined veterans admired by Frederick the Great, including the vaunted "Black Watch" of the British army, the terror of Europe.

They fought bravely.

Gilbert de Motier, Marquis de Lafayette, (1757-1834), symbol of the all-important French millions and ships, chased Benedict Arnold through Maryland in 1781, stayed on for the final triumph on the Chesapeake. (WAG)

General William Smallwood (EPFL)

Rallying points and rescues

Maryland troops were in the field before the Declaration of Independence and the Continental Congress was in Maryland only months after the ink on the declaration was dry.

Soon after the battle of Bunker Hill a detachment of volunteers, garbed in buckskin and led by Michael Cresap, a member of the paramount frontiersman dynasty of western Maryland, assembled first in Hagerstown and then in Frederick to go to the aid of hard-pressed Massachusetts. They marched 550 miles in 22 days.

By late summer of the next year, 1776, sizable Maryland forces under General William Smallwood had joined Washington's 9,500 troops on Long Island in what is now Brooklyn, N. Y. The British moved in for the first formal battle of the war.

Cornwallis hit hard, driving the poorly handled Americans back. A detachment of about 250 Marylanders made five suicidal charges at the Cortelyou house, a focal point for the battle, buying time so that Washington's main force and the rest of Smallwood's regiment could escape.

On December 12 of the same year, the Congress, frightened out of Philadelphia by the growing British threat, moved to Congress Hall, Baltimore. Two days after Christmas, they granted Washington virtually dictatorial powers, freedom to hire and fire and "arrest the disaffected."

Market square, Hagerstown, about 1773. (EPFL)

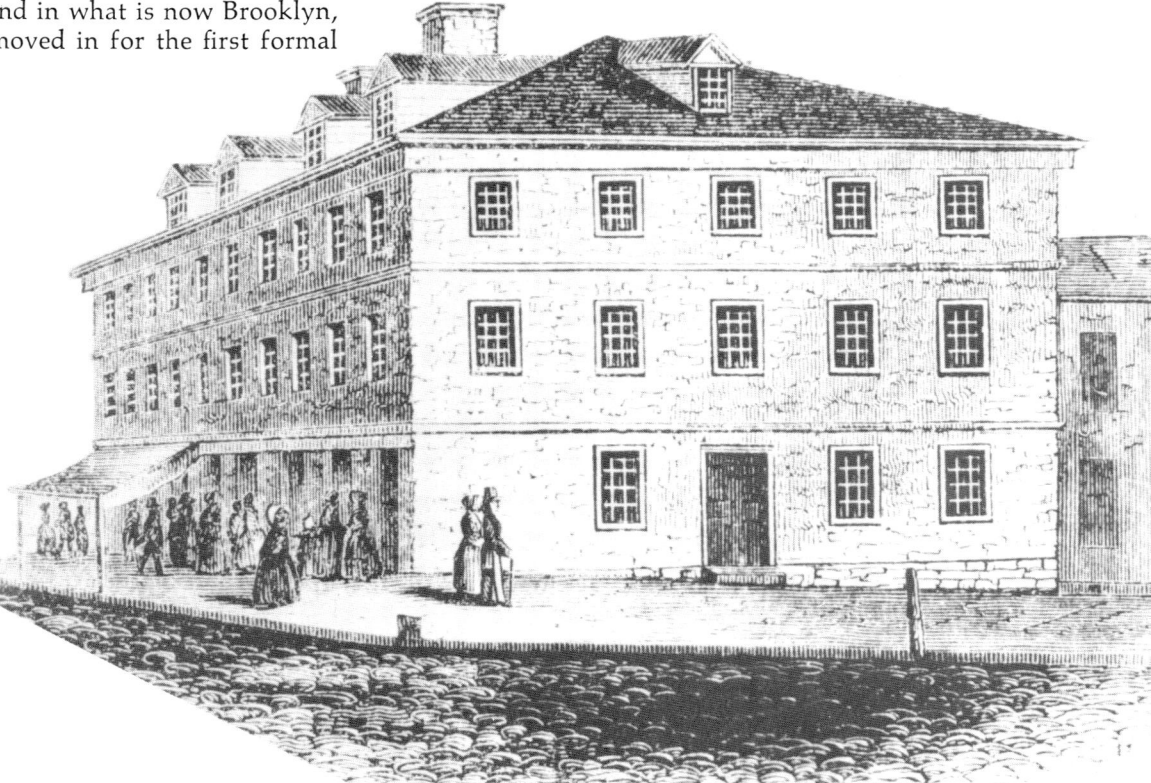

Congress Hall, home of a harried gathering. (EPFL)

The fatal step

"England hath given her warning to depart. O receive the fugitive, and prepare in time an asylum for mankind."
                                    Thomas Paine

To the hard-bitten, professional revolutionaries of New England, who had been knee-deep in what King George regarded as treason for about a decade, the men from Maryland on these pages seemed indolent and almost unconcerned.

The delegation that turned up in Philadelphia in the summer of 1776 to sign the Declaration of Independence was, however, a remarkably well-balanced one in terms of the way it represented Maryland interests.

There was mild-mannered Thomas Stone, gentleman farmer who has left few marks on history other than a beautiful home, "Habre de Venture," near Port Tobacco.

There was the great landholder, Charles Carroll of Carrollton, whose holdings were equalled only by a handful of Hudson river barons and the grandees of Virginia and South Carolina.

There was the "city man", urbane and up to his neck in politics, able William Paca and there was the jurist personified in the form of Samuel Chase, ruddy-faced, outspoken and without thought of consequence for his personal safety as he was to prove when impeached, and acquitted as Justice of the United States under Thomas Jefferson.

Lieut. Col. Nathaniel Ramsey and the 3rd Maryland regiment stemmed the tide of retreat at Monmouth, N. J., last major battle of the northern campaign and the site of Washington's famous rebuke to General Charles Lee for cowardice. (EPFL)

The scene at Cortelyou farm, where the Maryland troops bought time. Watching with a glass, Washington said: "Good God! What brave fellows I must this day lose!" (EPFL)

The southern struggle

As the war shifted to the south, so did Maryland commanders and their followers.

Massive British forces executed a huge loop through the Carolinas after the fall of Charleston.

In nearly every major engagement, Maryland men and commanders were involved.

Most dazzling engagement was the battle of Cowpens, S. C., where the fiery Britisher, Banastre Tarleton, attempted to force the continentals back to King's Mountain, near Charlotte.

A tremendous clash of royal fusiliers and Maryland and Delaware troops occurred, with John Eager Howard shouting "Give them the bayonet!" It was the brightest, and one of the only, American victories of the long southern fight.

Later Otho H. Williams screened the main continental force for an escape into North Carolina and also played a leading role in the battle of Eutaw Springs, where General Greene lost one fourth of his active troops.

A powerful force in supporting the Constitution was Charles Carroll of Carrollton, (1737-1832). (MHS)

John Eager Howard. (EPFL)

Thomas Stone of Charles county, (1743-1787), was the grandson of a Colonial governor and lived quietly in the small, brilliant circle centering around Port Tobacco. (BMA)

Symbol of British Loyalty, Rev. Jonathan Boucher, an Annapolis minister and friend of George Washington. (BS)

Otho H. Williams. (EPFL)

London-educated William Paca, (1740-1799), of Harford county was Maryland governor under the Articles of Confederation. (MHS)

Samuel Chase of Somerset, (1741-1811), was the prime mover in getting Maryland's approval of the revolutionary drift to Philadelphia. (MHS)

Mordecai Gist's Marylanders moved into the Carolinas for mopping up campaigns after Yorktown. (EPFL)

A depiction of the battle of Cowpens, lonely American victory. (EPFL)

The Gray's Inn Creek shipyard of Capt. Lambert Wickes was one of the many Maryland slips that built privateers in the sea effort. (MHS)

The final effort

Though ravaged by inflation, Maryland responded quickly to the closing phases of the war. James Calhoun, of Baltimore, was deputy postmaster general for western Maryland, and headed the effort to assemble, lumber, cannon, food, blankets and military necessities for the outpouring of Continentals and their baggage trains.

James Calhoun (MHS)

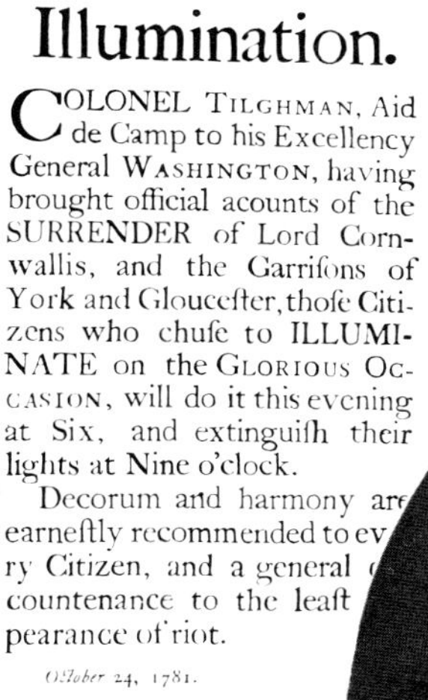

Tench's ride

In October of 1781, with the help of a French fleet, allied forces bottled up about 8,000 soldiers and sailors under Lord Cornwallis on Virginia's Yorktown peninsula.

The siege was a short-range affair and by October 18 the British forces were marching out to surrender, playing the air "The World Turned Upside Down."

At George Washington's side were Gen. Mordecai Gist and Lieut. Col. Tench Tilghman, along with about 1,000 troops of the 3rd and 4th Maryland regiments, about one-ninth of the American troops at the triumph.

Tench began his famous ride, second only to Paul Revere's gallop, though it was partly by water. The destination was the Congress in Philadelphia. Another messenger beat him to Annapolis, but he pounded northward.

He reached the federal capital early on the morning of October 22. Each member of congress contributed a dollar out of his own pocket for traveling expenses of Col. Tilghman.

Illumination.

COLONEL TILGHMAN, Aid de Camp to his Excellency General WASHINGTON, having brought official acounts of the SURRENDER of Lord Cornwallis, and the Garrisons of York and Gloucester, those Citizens who chuse to ILLUMINATE on the GLORIOUS OCCASION, will do it this evening at Six, and extinguish their lights at Nine o'clock.

Decorum and harmony are earnestly recommended to every Citizen, and a general countenance to the least appearance of riot.

October 24, 1781.

Avoid a riot, the poster cautioned. (EPFL)

Tench Tilghman (EPFL)

The state house, Annapolis, in its early days, scene of Washington's tear-stained resignation as commander in chief. (EPFL)

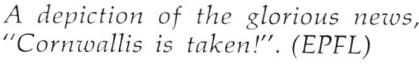

A depiction of the glorious news, "Cornwallis is taken!". (EPFL)

'A fund of public virtue'

Looking back on the turbulent tale, John Hanson, the Frederick county leader, saw it as a distinct landfall in human history. He had this stately epitaph for the crucial years...

Bohemia Manor, the Milligan seat in Cecil county. The British looted and burned nearby on the way to the battle of Brandywine in 1777. (AAB)

Hessian barracks, Frederick, favorite lockup for redcoats who got caught by the continentals. (AAB)

"During the whole memorable interval between the fall of the old and the institution of the new form of government, there appeared to exist amongst us such a fund of public virtue as has scarcely a parallel in the annals of the world." (BMA)

1783 GOLD AND GLORY 1814

THE GRUELLING AND anti-climactic American Revolution left Maryland financially broke and divided into factions, uncertain of the role of the new national government and the state's part in it. With almost no claims to western lands, the state had some affinity with the smaller states of the new nation, and less with the mighty seats of power, Virginia, New York and Pennsylvania. Yet, with a population approaching 400,000, and a far more complex economic structure than most southern states, Maryland had a community of interest, too, with the rising commercial states.

Eastern Maryland expressed its opposition early to paying for the vaunted "internal improvements" that were increasingly demanded by the growth of the grain trade and the rise of marketing towns.

The fact was that most segments of the state economy were in shambles. Rich men had been ruined; there were clamors for debt payment on all sides. Hard coin vanished overnight.

Baltimore narrowly missed being selected the national capital early in the era, but muffed it when a deal with New York fell through. This was to have a memorable sequel a few years later when Benjamin Banneker, eminent black surveyor-scientist of Maryland was selected to lay out the city of Washington on Maryland land.

The era brought the first generation of municipal architects to the Chesapeake shores and soon the most important of them had created major styles that were to last through the Nineteenth Century.

With the revolutionary ordeal over, religious elements in the state began major organizational efforts, founding landmark churches and systems that survive to this day and tapped the continuing spirit of the "great awakening", the Eighteenth Century's remarkable urban revival.

Harassments at sea during the Napoleonic era plagued commerce and ruined some Marylanders as the federal era progressed and in 1797 the government launched the U. S. Frigate *Constellation*, pride of the state at a cost of over $314,000. (It survives as a Baltimore harbor attraction.)

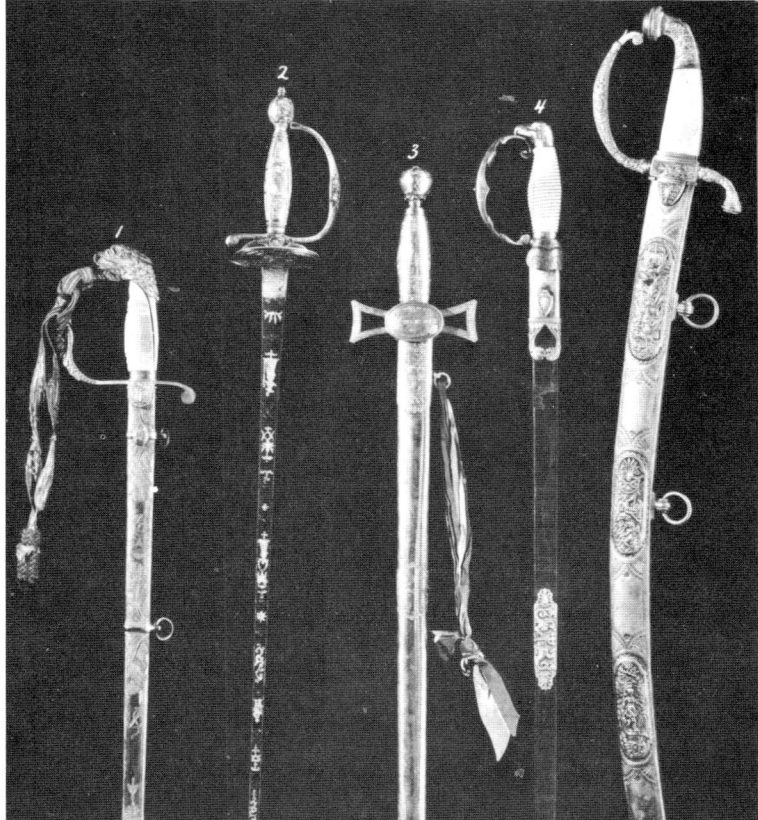

Some ceremonial swords of early Nineteenth Century Maryland warriors. General Sam Smith's is fourth from the left. (EPFL)

A native of Prince Georges county, John Thomas Clagett, (1742-1816) became the first Episcopal Bishop of Maryland. (EPFL)

Archbishop John Carroll, (1735-1815), headed the nation's Catholic life for the first quarter century of the United States. The Upper Marlboro native spoke four languages and founded Georgetown University (EPFL)

There was a surge of growth westward and the United States population center moved 42 miles in that direction across the state in 10 years, beginning a march toward the middle west.

The choppy early federal era did not prevent the state from advancing and experimenting. In 1794 at Bladensburg the first balloon ascent occurred with a 13-year-old Baltimore boy handling the ropes. Glass manufacturing made its debut in western Maryland and road rolling on a scientific scale made its bow in 1810 on the York road, Baltimore county.

Robert Carey Long designed the Peale Museum, first building designed as a public museum in the United States. It opened in August, 1814. Gas as illumination was demonstrated in 1802 along Baltimore's Water street.

These early stirrings were accompanied by a canterous political scene in which Maryland legal talent played major roles. The state came closer to abolishing slavery than at any time before the great conflict of 1861-1865. It was proposed as early as 1789 by Charles Carroll of Carrollton. Religious divines, especially of Methodist persuasion, thundered against the practice, which was gradually yielding to manumission.

In April of 1814, the Emperor Napoleon abdicated after keeping Europe in an uproar for 17 years. This left the mighty British naval establishment free to bring full power against America and the Chesapeake Bay. They proceeded to do it with dispatch.

Stirrings of faith

These people and places figured in the extension of faith and freedom in the state's earliest days as a state, leading to national reputations and in one case, international accolade.

Freeborn Garrettson, Maryland Methodist minister, freed his slaves, crusaded in the south, preaching to blacks and urging abolition. (AC)

A Baptism in Baltimore's Jones Falls during the early days. (PM)

Aristocratic Elizabeth Ann Bayley Seton, (1744-1821), founded 20 communities of the Sisters of Charity from a nucleus at Emmitsburg, Carroll county and was canonized by the Catholic church in 1975. (EPFL)

Lovely Lane meeting house, Baltimore, where Francis Asbury was chosen first bishop of the Methodist Church in America at an 1784 conference. (EPFL)

James McHenry (1753-1818) (MHS)

*Men of mark in the early years
. . . a gallery*

These Maryland men were important forces in their day in the shaping of the new republic.

Luther Martin (1748-1826) (LC)

Bladensburg attorney William Wirt first came to national prominence in the trial of Aaron Burr, was a powerful author-politician, three-time U. S. attorney general and romanticizer of the life of Patrick Henry. Implacable foe of Thomas Jefferson and Maryland's first attorney general, Martin opposed the Constitution and was involved in both the Justice Chase and Burr trials. Pinkney, the number one orator of the federal period, argued 71 cases before the Supreme Court and supported the abolition of slavery in 1789, changed his tune in 1820 by backing the Missouri Compromise creating a new slave state. Irish-born Maryland immigrant, James McHenry did yoeman service in the revolution as Washington's aide and was a signer of the Constitution. Appointed Secretary of War in 1796, he was caught in the crossfire of the federalist feuds, called out of a dinner party in May, 1800 and virtually forced to resign by cantankerous President John Adams.

William Wirt (1772-1834) (LC)

William Pinkney (1764-1822) (LC)

France sets the fate for three

The turbulent federal period was even more fun in France and acts of the French republic had a decided effect on the fate of these three Marylanders. One got money, one lost it and a third went to Paris.

Betsy Patterson, beautious daughter of one of Baltimore's wealthier merchant princes, married Jerome Bonaparte, younger brother of the French first consul, was disavowed by the Bonapartes, pensioned by France and survived into the 1870's, collecting her own ground rents in person by hired hack. (EPFL)

William Vans Murray, ardent federalist, figured in one of the most famous brou-ha-has in American diplomatic history. He was suddenly named minister to France by John Adams in response to feelers from wily Talleyrand, the French diplomatist who wanted to settle the trouble with the United States. Murray, then Dutch Ambassador, was demoted to a mere commission member, but got to Paris, anyway. (ML)

French seizures of ships at sea during the "undeclared war" with France at the turn of the Nineteenth Century broke the financial back of wealthy merchant ship owner, Thorowgood Smith. In 1800 he was forced to sell everything, including the house. (EPFL)

A souvenir of the French troubles, sheet music published honoring the U. S. Frigate Constellation. *She captured the French ship* Insurgente *off Nevis in 1799, next year mauled* La Vengeance, *a French vessel of war (LC)*

Designs for the new republic

The mechanic arts and public works were all the rage during the rare intervals of peace. The federal era marks the beginning of a distinguished chain of designers who started changing the face of Maryland.

Maximilien Godefroy inaugurated the Gothic revival in America with this distinguished design for the Chapel of the Presentation of the Blessed Virgin Mary in Baltimore. (AAB)

Maryland's first state seal, rendered by John Barber. (DB)

James Rumsey, a Cecil countian, mounted this steamboat model and made it move in 1787 on the Potomac river, far ante-dating the widely publicized Robert Fulton tests. It failed to catch on and the inventor died five years after the debut. (EPFL)

Frederick county landmark, Jug bridge, rose in 1808 to carry the eastern leg of the National Road. It collapsed in 1942. The Jug remains, its significance a mystery (MDT)

The Baltimore Cathedral, masterpiece of Benjamin Latrobe, an architect also of the U. S. Capitol, in its early days. (EPFL)

The "telescope" house, built in stages as the affluence of Maryland planters increased, became a classic and model for Kentucky, Missouri architecture. This is Southern Maryland's Mount Republican, built in 1792. (AAB)

A top tourist attraction in its day, the Maryland penitentiary, Baltimore, sketched by Latrobe. (EPFL)

Maryland fights a war . . . and wins one!

In 1812, James Madison and his advisors—fed up with years of high-handed acts and seizures at sea and with years of playing Britain against France and vice versa—unwisely declared war on the former.

Britain mounted an immediate, highly effective embargo and blockade, sweeping U. S. interests from the seas. Empire forces moved in on large swaths of the American frontier and Indians rose in force, on the British side.

In August of 1814, a British fleet force staffed with Wellington's veterans sailed up the Patuxent river, landed at Benedict and at Bladensburg shattered a far larger and hastily-assembled militia army, including the Baltimore artillery. In a vengeful lunge, the redcoats burned the White House and the Capitol building, amid local panic and widespread looting.

Baltimore's turn was next. By September 1 its streets were alive with the rumble of wagons and coaches as citizens sprang to the alarm. Cash and valuables by the carvan-load left for York, Pa. General Sam Smith, a 62-year-old Revolutionary veteran took over and assembled about 17,000 vounteers, including Hagerstown and Pennsylvania foot soldiers.

Bane of the British Navy for 40 years was the great Maryland naval commander, Joshua Barney, (1759-1818). Captured three times and jailed once during the Revolution, he jumped back into the fray at Bladensburg, was bagged by the British for the fourth time. (PM)

Defenders swept across this Jones Falls bridge, moving southeast to meet the British onslaught. (MHS)

Far from all the British effort was concentrated on Baltimore and vicinity. These people and places figured in the short and, in the end, indecisive conflict.

Raiders assaulted the Eastern Shore and other Bay points but the Americans chalked up a victory at Moorefields when they fought off and killed Sir Peter Parker, captain of the **Menelaus** expedition into the Bay. British soldiers stabled their horses in Christ Church, Chaptico, St. Marys county. (EPFL)

Roughest Indian foe for America was Tecumseh, (1768-1813). He earned this lasting memorial on the Naval Academy grounds in the form of the figurehead from the bowsprit of the U. S. S. Delaware. (AAB)

Nathan Towson, (1784-1854), popular attack captain, captured the British brig **Caledonia**, while it was under the guns of Fort Erie in October, 1812. (MHS)

Cambridge, a vulnerable village, as it looked a few years before the British invasion. (EPFL)

The city rallies

Baltimore had a record of being feisty and sometimes ferocious. As the war opened, a mob sacked the offices of an anti-Madison journal and besieged federalist General Henry Lee, attacking a jail and killing one person and seriously crippling others. It was defiant, if impractical and *Niles Weekly Register*, an influential national journal published in the city, predicted an Irish uprising if Britain attacked America.

Nothing like that happened. The well-equipped Britishers looped around Southern Maryland, scaring the daylights out of a defenseless Annapolis, entering the Patapsco and unloading nearly 5,000 troops of the line at North Point for a march northwestward toward the city.

On September 12, the British met Baltimore's outer defenses at the narrowest point of the Patapsco neck and badly shattered the raw

Troops assemble for the North Point fight. (MHS)

levies of General John Stricker. By a quirk, however, someone (possibly two saddler's apprentices named Daniel Wells and Henry McComas) shot the British field commander General Robert Ross. This broke the spirit of the British in continuing the land assault, though they had reached a point just a few miles from the city.

"I'll dine tonight in Baltimore—or in hell!" said British General Ross after a breakfast at the Gorsuch farm en route to the North Point fight. A volley from General Stricker's advance party settled the question. (EPFL)

Meanwhile the British sea force had moved within a few miles of Fort McHenry, bastion of the inner harbor, flanked by block ships that closed the northwest branch leading to the downtown.

A few miles below the assault force on a British craft was Georgetown lawyer, Francis Scott Key, on a mission intended to free a friend, Dr. William Beanes, of Upper Marlboro, who had been imprisoned by the British for alleged breach of trust.

High above the fort flew a huge American flag, 30 by 42 feet made by Mary Pickersgill, an east Baltimore maker of merchant flags.

Most of September 13, the British shelled the fort unmolested by the out-of-range guns of the Americans. The bombships continued their cannonade through the night, firing 200-pound shells and Congreve rockets. Sometime after sunrise, 5.50 A. M., Francis Scott Key raised a spyglass on the deck of the truce ship. The flag was still there.

The North Point fight as a contemporary artist saw it. The 27th regiment is in the foregound under the trees. (EPFL)

General Sam Smith, leader of the Baltimore defense. (EPFL)

His elegant suburban home, "Montebello." (EPFL)

The Star-Spangled-Banner in its magnificent Smithsonian Institution setting. (SI)

It was September 16 before Key was released from his truce ship with Dr. Beanes. Soon his anthem was struck off as a handbill, set to the music of an English drinking air, "Anacreon in Heaven," and spread, rather slowly at first, across the nation. Key did not name his big moment; the title came from the poem that came from the flag.

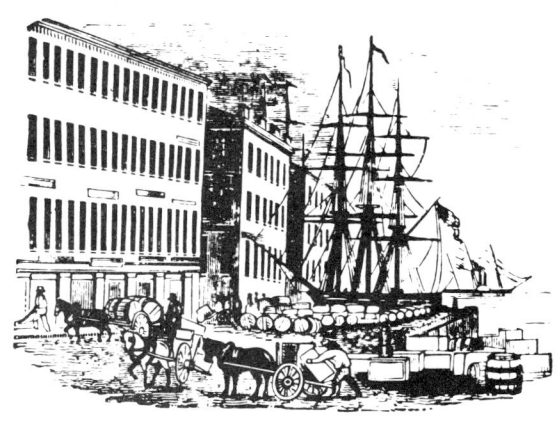

A dockside scene of the early Republic.

A mock bombardment of Fort McHenry, restaged during the "good old days." (LC)

A contemporary rendition of the bombardment (MHS)

Francis Scott Key (MHS)

The flag house, where Mary Pickersgill made the flag. (FA)

A cartoon hailing the British defeat. John Bull is showing taking his licks from Baltimore and crying "Mercy . . . mercy on me!" (EPFL)

Key's first manuscript copy in the Maryland Historical Society (MHS)

"Key's key to the city," a mid-1930's tribute to the Star Spangled Banner and its author, made from a joist of the Flag House and adorned with the author's portrait. (EPFL)

1814 — 1860
LAVENDER AND LAMPLIGHT

ANTE-BELLUM MARYLAND cared about making itself important, in trade, politics and the arts.

There was a spirit of cooperation between the planter class, the merchants and the bright new legal talents that were rising in Annapolis, Baltimore and other centers. Their unity of approach was remarkable for a divisive period.

As a result, accompanied by outlandish political maneuvering and even fraud, Maryland literally borrowed itself into bankruptcy, churning out more than $14 million in subsidies and favors for public works at a time when its annual income was probably less than that of John Jacob Astor, the New York tycoon.

The results, even so, were dazzling. Within a short time there were at least a half-dozen achievements of major import to the western world created in Maryland.

The Maryland "team", if that is the word, launched the historic Baltimore & Ohio railroad westward, the nation's first large scale railroad operation.

It started work on the Chesapeake & Ohio Canal, to tap the rich coals of Western Maryland.

The first corporate-municipal gas lighting in the world was inaugurated in Baltimore at a point when most European cities were murky masterpieces by night.

Well-engineered roadbuilding surfaced in the central state and the first use of durable, macadam pikes.

Baltimore Clippers, well underway as a trade weapon in the early federal period, continued to set speed records world-wide that were simply not believed in the exchanges of Liverpool and London. (The ships proved impractical as long-range shippers, were converted to the slave trade.)

The first electronic "scoop" in world newspaper history was scored in 1844. Samuel F. B. Morse, laying his telegraph lines along the Baltimore-Washington B&O route, sent the famous message, "What hath God wrought" to the amazed dignitaries at Mount Clare station, Baltimore. Back over the line a few weeks later went the news of the nomination of Henry Clay for president, beating reporters back to Washington by two hours.

Many of these internal improvements aroused the ire of the isolated, wholly agricultural Eastern Shore, but they helped part of the western state and by 1836 vast Frederick county was ready to be subdivided into Frederick and Carroll counties. Baltimore continued to reinforce its reputation as "mobtown" through a

Beautiful Olney, Harford county, the epitome of Greek Revival classicism and "away down South in Dixie"—Maryland style. (EPFL)

series of pitched battles between fire companies, a banking riot and the bloody elections of the 1850's which featured skirmishes between saloon gangs like the "blood tubs" and the "plug uglies."

The commercial capital, however, was helpful in other ways and the huge cottom boom of the flush 1840's, and Baltimore's role in it, helped bail out the creaky, outlandishly overdrawn government in Annapolis. By 1846, one could get from the Bay region to New York city in 16 hours, using a boat-train combination and the telegraph was to make families and towns that were weeks or months apart, only hours distant.

Sizzling technologies surfaced and Maryland lumberyards built whole towns worth of buildings, houses and saloons in prefab style, shipped them around South America to feed the California gold rush.

Politically the state was dominated to a degree by eastern and southern Maryland, an area that chose half the Maryland senate while it had only half the population of the rest of the state. Slave population was dropping and the state, by 1860, had one fifth of the 500,000 free negroes in the United States, with nearly one third of these Maryland blacks housed in and around Baltimore.

Marylanders were not wholly indifferent to black welfare. Elisha Tyson, of Baltimore, was a pioneer in the new wave of interest in abolition and Moses Sheppard, a wealthy Quaker who died in 1857, worked for the purposes of the American Colonization Society.

Loneliest of all the foes of the status quo was William Gunnison, a virtually penniless, ex-merchant and "free-soiler" who became the town crank of Baltimore in the 1850's, pestering the mighty with calls for immediate emancipation. He died, ignored by the Republican party, in 1892.

Maryland was not very effective or even consistent in trying to find an answer to the great moral maze of slavery. The answer, it was soon to discover, was guns.

Banks, politics . . . and angry Andy

The big stories of Maryland's second post-war era centered around banks, politics and Andrew Jackson.

Before the state could catch its breath from the trade wars of the Napoleonic period, it was knee-deep in a seismic court case involving finance.

James McCulloch, a Baltimore bank cashier who had lent himself $500,000 according to at least one authority, refused to pay a $15,000 Maryland tax bill on the bank.

Maryland lost. The unanimous decision before John Marshall, *McCulloch vs. Maryland*, upheld federal rights of incorporation and denied to the states the right to interfere in taxation. A little over a decade later, the great battle between Andrew Jackson and the Bank of the United States and its leadership, headed by Nicholas Biddle, drew Maryland into its stormy orbit. Jackson and his attorney general, Roger Brooke Taney, of Maryland, worked out a plan for stripping the Philadelphia-dominated bank of its power by transferring to the famous "pet banks."

James McCulloch (EPFL)

Science, society and the social graces

In the early days of the Nineteenth Century, everything was "correct". Ladies and gentlemen attended jousting tourneys in the countryside, viewed the new works in the Maryland Institute's Baltimore palace, bought elegant "albums" from printer Fielding Lucas and, if male, attended lengthy and sometimes historic bashes in Baltimore hostelries. The military air was favored.

The wealthy mill-owning Ellicotts controlled the Union Bank, recipient of Andrew Jackson's favors. The "pet bank" was housed in this superb building by Robert Carey Long. (EPFL)

"Gentlemen, I shall be glad to see this mob on Capitol Hill. The leaders I will hang as high as Haman to deter forever all attempts to control the congress by intimidation!" Quote: Andrew Jackson when told that a Baltimore mob was headed his way to besiege Congress in support of the hated Bank of the United States. (EPFL)

Three-time Governor Charles C. Ridgely displays his riding form aboard "Tuckahoe." (EPFL)

Financial panics like the one in 1837 generated small change famines and paper coins, like this 25c scrip were issued. (EPFL)

A memento of Maryland's traditional ring tourneys, reviving medieval gallantry—all the rage in the 1840's at White Sulphur Springs, Va., and silhouetted here on William Gilmore's York road estate. The lady love waits at right for the champ. (EPFL)

The militant air of the forties, a gathering of Hagerstown, New Market and other Western Maryland militia in 1843. (MHS)

Marvels of the horsedrawn age

Booming population and trade put strains on the state's ability to deliver the goods, especially in competition with northern centers. These scenes show some of the technological marvels designed to help out during the "manifest destiny" period.

Launched the same day, but never as successful was the C&O Canal, shown here in a Nineteenth century view when the 184-mile route was still operating. (EPFL)

With the help of a $500,000 state loan and a spadeful of dirt from Charles Carroll of Carrollton, last of the signers and shown here with the shovel, the Baltimore and Ohio railroad is launched at Mount Clare, July 4, 1828. (BORRM)

An earlier view of the canal in about 1865. (LC)

A 20-foot wide macadam turnpike, 15 inches deep at the center and 10.5 miles long was a national "first" when built in 1823. (MDT)

Route of the Boonsboro-Hagerstown pioneering road. (MDT)

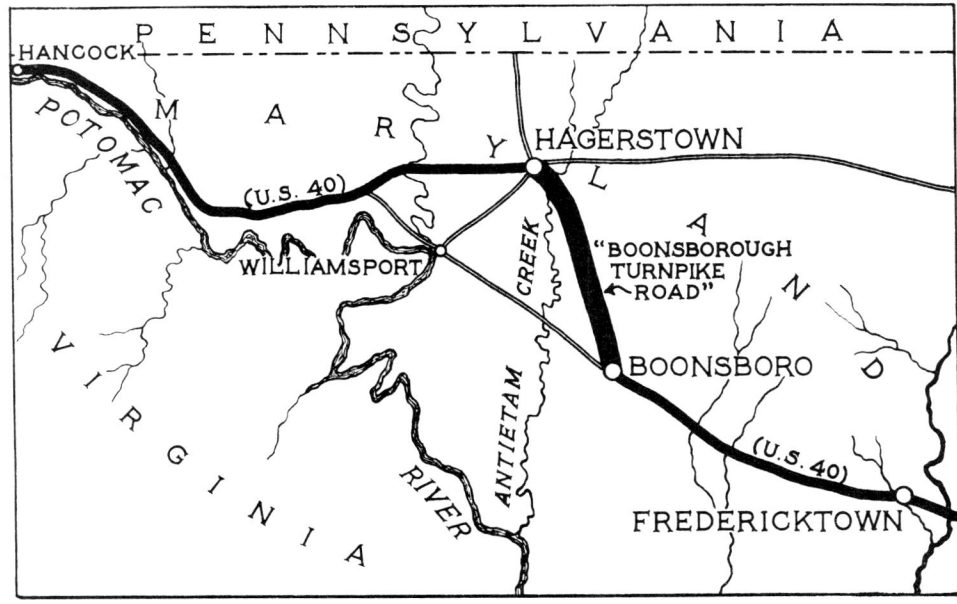

RATES of TOLL

For every Score of Sheep	4 Cents
of Hogs	4 Do
of Cattle	8 do
Every Horse & Rider or led Horse	2 do
Every Chair, or Chaise, with one Horse & two Wheels	4 do
Every Carriage or Waggon with two Horses & four Wheels	8 do
For the same, with four Horses	12 do
Every Cart or Waggon, narrow tire For each Horse drawing the same	4 do
Every Cart or Waggon broad tread, Each Horse drawing the same	2 do
Two Oxen in draft equal to one Horse.	
Every Mule equal to one Horse.	

Sheep were cheaper than cows and four-horse carriages cost more than either. Maryland made the National Road a toll facility in 1835. (MDT)

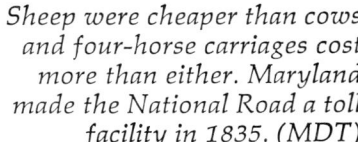

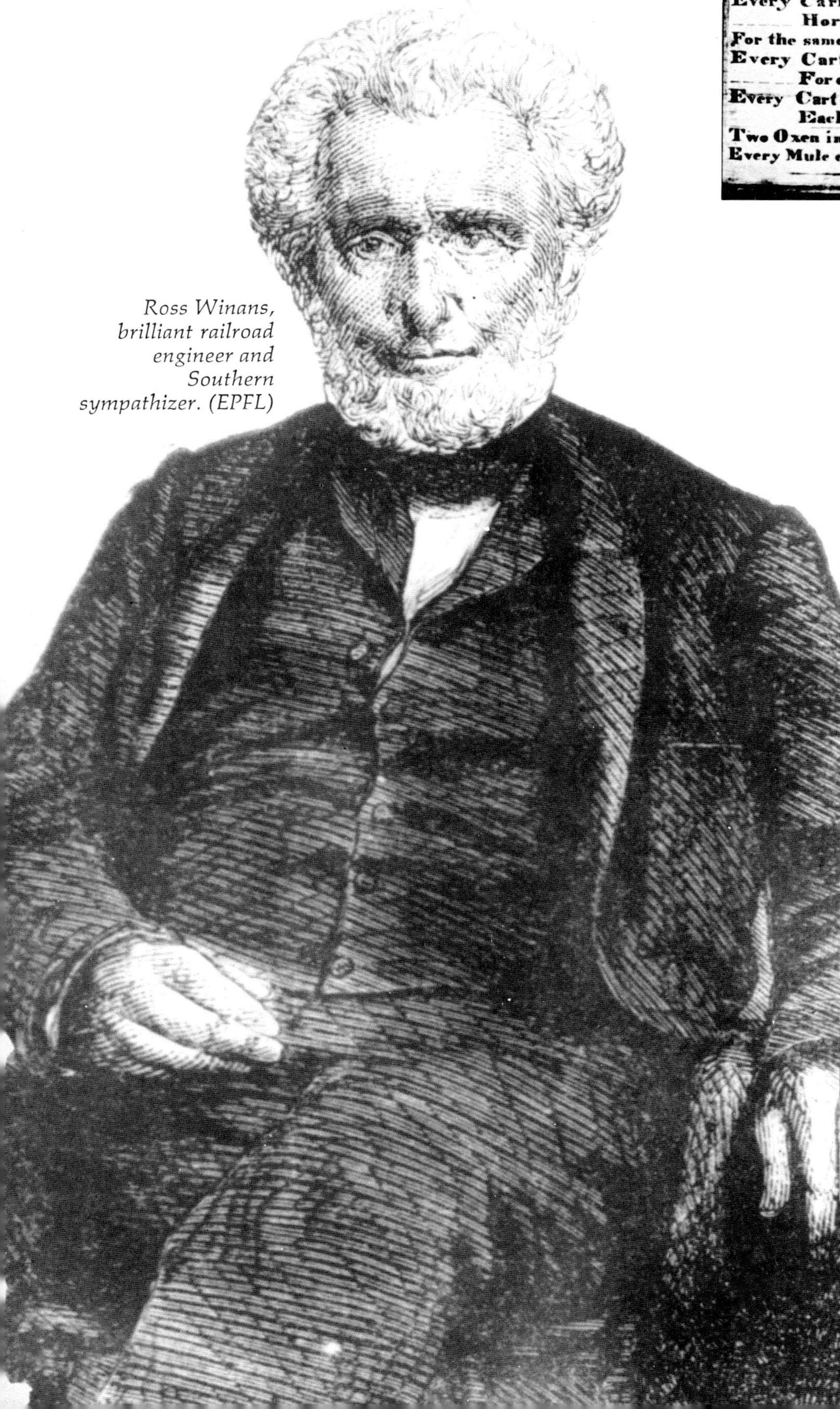

Ross Winans, brilliant railroad engineer and Southern sympathizer. (EPFL)

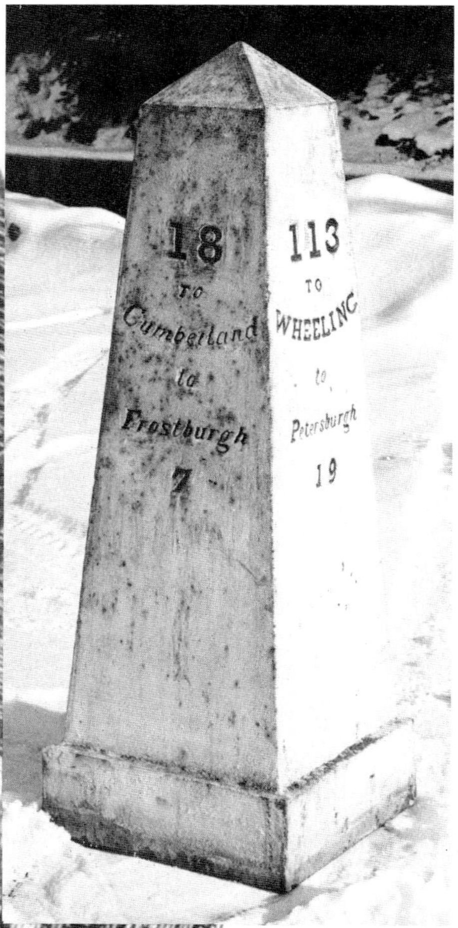

Stone markers for travelers along the National Road west were guideposts. This one from west of Frostburg is now in the Smithsonian Institution. (MDT)

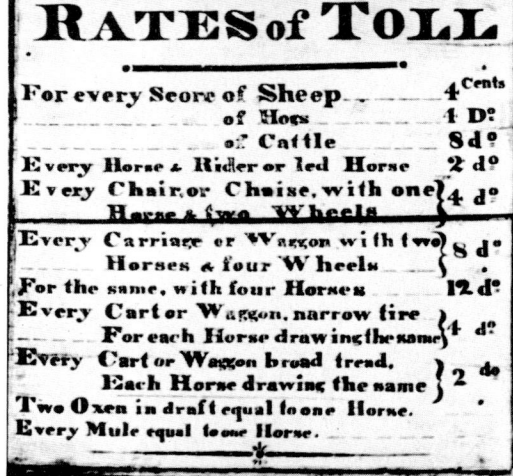

Mr. Winans' strange "cigar boat" had them gaping when it made trial runs with four engines and powered flanges amidship. The novelty wore off, the cigar fizzled and the submarine came later. (EPFL)

Rembrandt Peale announces the arrival of the gaslit age in a demonstration at his museum in June, 1816. The new system lit up the Baltimore city council, too. A few days later they chartered the Baltimore Gas Light Company, first in the nation. (BGE)

The Fairview Inn on the National Pike westward, a favorite stopover spot for travelers. (MHS)

Some ante-bellum sensations

Blood and thunder, on and off stage, were features of the late Federal and Jacksonian periods and in Maryland everyone kept a weather eye on their money in the bank and their lottery tickets. Speed records and bootleg prize fights, illegal, but held on the Eastern Shore, were other attractions.

The world marveled at the speed of the Baltimore clippers, including the Mary Whitridge. She cleared the Atlantic in a record 13.5 days, here has heavy going against a China Seas typhoon. (EPFL)

No. 1 Maryland hero, Eastern Shoreman Stephen Decatur, (1779-1820), had bearded the bashaw of Tripoli and the dey of Algiers in their dens but was shot dead in a Bladensburg duel by an associate. (EPFL)

Yankee Sullivan and Tom Hyer square off on Kent Island in 1819 for a $10,000 purse. Hyer won in 10 rounds. (MHS)

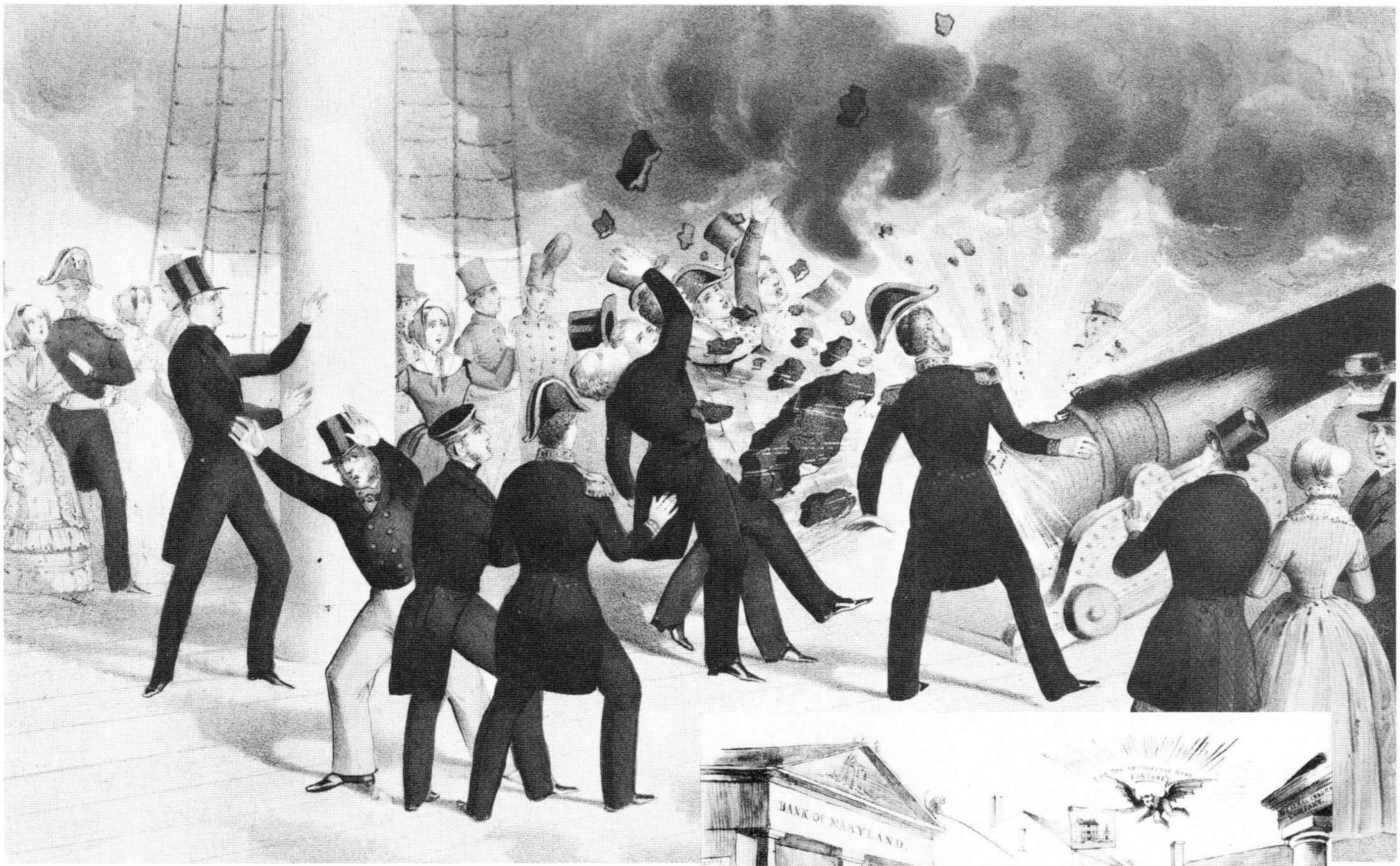

Civilians and two cabinet ministers died in a sudden gun explosion aboard the S. S. Princeton, *a Potomac tragedy of 1844. (LC)*

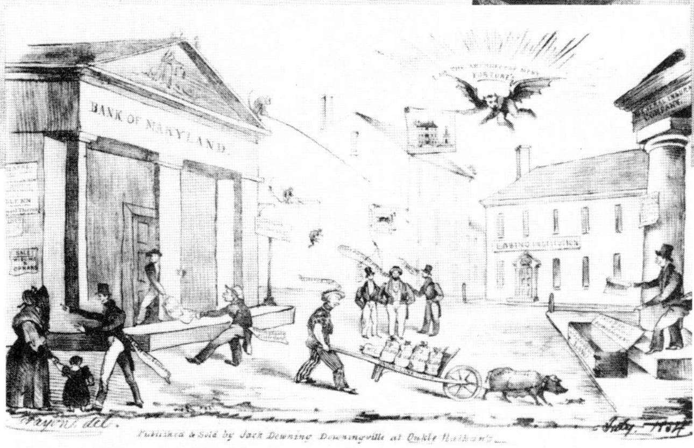

A Downing print memorializes the Bank of Maryland failure in the 1830's. (MHS)

CONINE'S Lottery Office

BALTIMORE, MARCH 8, 1825.

Maryland State Lottery,

NO. III.

☞Highest prize $40,000.—The payment of all prizes guaranteed by the State.

Original Scheme.

TO BE COMPLETED IN TWENTY DRAWINGS.

1	prize of	$40,000	is	$40,000
1	do.	20,000		20,000
1	do.	10,000		10,000
2	do.	5,000		10,000
30	do.	1,000		30,000
20	do.	500		10,000
50	do.	100		5,000
100	do.	50		5,000
5000	do.	10		50,000

5205 Prizes—14,795 Blanks. $180,000

☞ Prizes subject to a deduction of 15 per cent. payable in 60 days after the drawing is finished.

The drawings are conducted under the superintendence of the Commissioners appointed by the state.

☞PRESENT STATE.

Sixteen drawings over—only four remain—and all of the following prizes still undrawn!

1	prize of	$40,000	is	$40,000
1	do.	20,000	-	20,000
1	do.	10,000	-	10,000
1	do.	5,000	-	5,000
12	do.	1,000	-	12,000
6	do.	500	-	3,000
13	do.	100	-	1,300
51	do.	50	-	2,550
1919	do.	10	-	19,190

Amounting to $113,040

☞ DRAWING.—All the prizes are now in the wheel floating except the $40,000, which will be deposited on the opening of the wheel, for the 19th day's drawing, to take place on Wednesday, 30th inst. Should the $40,000 prize come out on the 19th drawing, the lottery will be completed the next day; if not, in order to afford opportunity for renewals, the *20th and last drawing* will be deferred to Tuesday, the 12th of April, when the lottery will positively be completed.

Whole Tickets, - $12 00; Halves, - - - - 6 00 } *Present Prices:* { Quarters, - - - $3 00; Eighths, - - - - 1 50

Tickets and Shares,

In the greatest variety of numbers, warranted undrawn, for sale at

CONINE'S OFFICE,

FORTUNE'S HOME, NO. 32, MARKET ST. BALTIMORE,

Who has had the pleasure lately of selling and paying to his customers, prizes to the amount of SEVERAL HUNDRED THOUSAND DOLLARS.

☞ As the tickets in the above brilliant lottery are rapidly going off, immediate purchases are consequently recommended in order to prevent any disappointment in obtaining chances. ☞Remittances will not be invested unless when received the state of the wheels justify it, and returned on receipt, or if requested invested in other lotteries.

☞Such as have been denied a proportionate share of the favors of Fortune heretofore, are respectfully invited to make a trial in the above lottery at CONINE's office.

MATCHETT, PRINTER

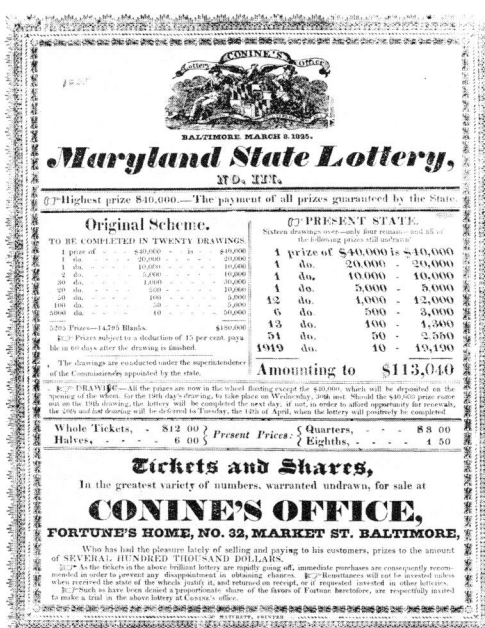

You had to play to win then, too. (MHS)

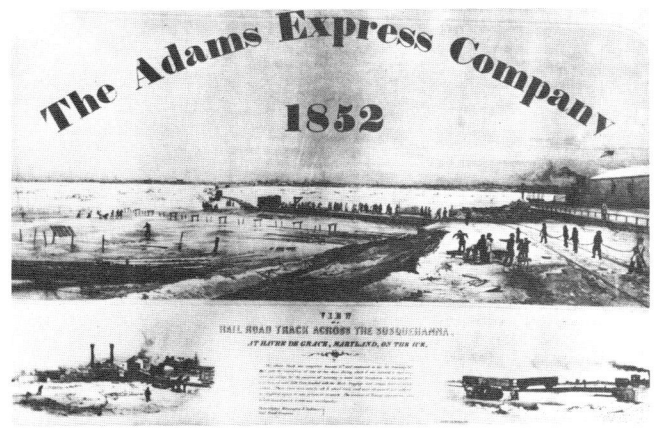

Tracks were laid across the river at Havre de Grace when the Susquehanna froze and the railroad advertised the fact in this poster. (EPFL)

Steps toward wider education

Attempts to organize a state-wide education system (including proposed fusion of St. John's College, Annapolis and Washington College, Chestertown) dated back almost to the Revolutionary era but always foundered on the shoals of politics.

This left education in Maryland largely in private hands, but this was the golden age of "academies" and the state became a national center for secondary schooling of young ladies.

Annapolis social life revived in 1845 with the establishment of Maryland's first really nationally-oriented institution, the United States Naval Academy.

A fashionable boy's school at mid-century. St. Timothy's, Catonsville, Baltimore county. (EPFL)

St. John's College in the mid fifties. (PM)

A vernal atmosphere, plus one of the nation's first direct passenger lines, made Ellicott City, and Patapsco Female Institute a popular Athens for young ladies, from 1840 well into the century. (BS)

An academy scene of 1854. (LC)

Downtown Baltimore as a London newspaper saw it in 1856. (LC)

Baltimore comes of age

In the post-War of 1812 period, Baltimore, already the state's largest population center, was also the nation's third largest city, attracting lecturers on the national orbit and in 1819 furnishing a platform for William Ellery Channing's famous statement of the Unitarian faith, delivered in a still-standing classic revival church by Maximilien Godefroy in downtown Baltimore.

Party conventions and New England businessmen piled into the booming center which by the 1850's had established dominance in the grain trade and virtually wrote the ticket for the eastern South commercially.

This is the Maryland praised by Charles Dickens, who liked the hotels, and by virtually all other outlanders, universal in their praise of the beauty of Maryland women and their stylish attire.

William Ellery Channing (LC)

A Whig party convention in 1840 at Canton Race course endorses John Tyler for president. (EPFL)

An 1850 view of Baltimore by Whitefield. (MHS)

Louis McLane, of Bohemia, Cecil county, took over the stalled B&O railroad from Betsy Patterson's brother, pushed it westwards from Harper's Ferry to Cumberland. (LC)

Peace and plenty

The growth of scientific agriculture, notably in the 1840's, and the use of fertilizer brought a new opulence, peace and plenty, to Maryland farm properties. Some scenes from that rural yesterday.

Clynmalira, the H. H. Carroll mansion at Sparks, Baltimore county, with unusual belvedered portico. (EPFL)

The Shriner Mill, near Frederick, ground up to 60 barrels of flour a day. It was built before 1820. (EPFL)

Mrs. Calvert's prize cow on her big spread at Riversdale. (ML)

CINDERELLA.
The property of C. B. Calvert, Esq. of Riversdale, Prince George's co. Md.

A poet dies

October, 1849 brought the end for the man who was probably the greatest literary talent with Maryland associations, Edgar Allan Poe, found virtually dead in a Baltimore saloon. He may have been a victim of "cooping" or the practice of dragging inebriates and mental cases from ward to ward in city elections and voting them illegally.

His later reputation suffered from an antagonistic biography by a northern literateur, Rufus Griswold. But Baltimore, except for its final abuse, had done well by the moody genius and the help extended early in his career by John Pendleton Kennedy, Maryland's important regional novelist, is one of the happier moments in American literary legend. Poe, through his stimulus to the great Symbolist movement in France, was the first American artist to influence world art, but he did more. His tragic and melodramatic tales continued the tradition of "Frankenstein" and led to the modern horror story. His "Gold Bug" did the same service for modern detective fiction, including the great treasure of Sherlock Holmes.

Poe's Amity street home before restoration. (EPFL)

Edgar Allan Poe (EPFL)

Church Home and Hospital, where the poet died, about a decade after his death. (EPFL)

Poe's grave in Westminster churchyard as it looked early in this century. (EPFL)

The Baltimore Poe knew, from a print of about 1845. (EPFL)

An affair of conscience

Slavery was unquestionably beginning to die out in Maryland by the 1850's. Vast stretches of southern Maryland and farms around Annapolis were vacated by planters as the land wore out and they moved on to the deep South. The Eastern Shore black was quite literally "half-slave and half-free" in terms of numbers. The same was true of Baltimore city's Negro population.

Maryland newspapers were crammed with notices of escaped slaves from the 1830's on. This early notice sought "Toby", a 14-year-old who risked capture unless he had "papers." (EPFL)

An abolitionist broadside, pleading for the black's condition. (LC)

In the wealthy Mount Vernon district in Baltimore there were only about 70 slaves serving the homes of the mighty.

Ironically, as the ancient bondage faded, slavery became a more and more destructive issue. Maryland voters witnessed the quick demise, in order, of the Whig party, of the antiforeign American ("Know Nothing") party and finally, the cataclysmic split of the Democrats.

In each case, the deepening outrage against chattel bondage made some contribution.

State legislators, dominated by rural interests, did nothing to change things. These people did.

Frederick Douglass, (1817-1895) born a Maryland slave, sponsored pray-ins, sit-ins and ride-ins in the North as war approached. His non-violent life theme was that change would come only when white hearts willed it. (MHS)

William Lloyd Garrison, (1805-1879) found out first hand how dangerous it was to criticize slavery when he wrote an inaccurate account of a Louisiana-bound slave cargo, was sued and locked up for 49 days in the Baltimore city jail. New England made him a martyr. (BS)

Beginning in 1849, Harriet Tubman, (1821-1913) started lofting more than 300 southern blacks to freedom in the north. A fearless captain of the underground railroad, she believed in abolition at any cost, supported John Brown's suicidal effort at Harper's Ferry. (BS)

Witnesses to disaster

Maryland found herself sharply at odds with national sentiment as the 1850's waned. Photography was then just new enough to capture some of these scenes.

For many, the times ahead would be difficult, tragic. Lincoln's election brought back into power the aggressive and potent Blair clan of Montgomery county. Montgomery Blair, however was to go into eclipse after the cataclism ahead, though he was virtual patronage king of the state as postmaster general. Henry Winter Davis was to die prematurely, at the peak of his powers and at a moment when his brilliance was sought to stabilize a turbulent time. Fate also earmarked Maryland's Gen. Henry Winder, C. S. A. He was to preside over the worst tragedy in American military history—the death of thousands of volunteers from disease and malnutrition at a place called Andersonville, Ga.

Heroes of 1814—Wells and McComas—lie in state in the Maryland Institute for reinterment at Monument and Gay street, Baltimore. (EPFL)

A Quaker party boards a Conestoga wagon for a bumpy trip to a meeting on the Gunpowder in 1859. (EPFL)

Maryland moderates were like the Millard Fillmore of this cartoon, accused of being "slaveholding villains" or "rascally abolitionists", depending on the point of view. (LC)

Dignified, able Mayor Thomas Swann presided over turbulent, disgracefully violent Baltimore elections in the late 1850's, was stripped of his police power by an angry General Assembly, creating a hiatus that outlasted more than a century. (EPFL)

A center for literary life, The Friday Club, enlivened the 1850's. At the far left is Henry Winter Davis, Republican notable with Severn T. Wallis on his left. George W. Dobbin is seated, center, behind the circular table. (EPFL)

The raid and execution of one-time Washington county resident, John Brown, widened the split in Maryland opinion and stimulated a field day for pro-Southern reaction. "Be quick," said the abolitionist hero to the hangman and the assembled troops, as a third-rate actor, John Wilkes Booth, serving in the Richmond Grays, hovered nearby. (LC)

1860 — 1865
THE FORGOTTEN ARSENAL

THE CIVIL WAR probably marks the nearest Maryland has come to anarchy since the religious upheavals of the Seventeenth Century.

Courts were restrained, newspapers suppressed, innocent people were locked up by the hundreds without charges and the squeeze of the state between joyous revolt in Virginia and the implacable determination of the North left Maryland almost alone in counseling moderation . . . negotiation.

Most border states were in the same corner. None, however, like Maryland, held the key to the nation's capital. The pikes of the state, the Bay and the Baltimore & Ohio railroad were the only link between Washington and the northern states. Lose this, thought the new Republican government, and we lose it all.

They were probably right. There is evidence that in 1862, as the Confederacy showed major signs of strength in invading the North, that the Prime Minister of England was getting ready to propose a joint recognition of the South in league with France.

It would have ruined the northern ports and perhaps brought on armed intervention of a sort which Napoleon III was fully capable, as he proved in Mexico. Luckily for the Union, the Southern withdrawal at Antietam cooled British ardor.

Maryland still had to face disastrous moral and economic issues. Trade declined. Millions in Southern trade balances vanished overnight. Families split up and in March of 1861, the Baltimore conference of the Methodist church voted itself independent of the northern fold. About 100 ministers and 12,000 churchmen, many of them Virginians, withdrew.

Stormy center of the Methodist Church split in the 1860's was Light Street Methodist Church in Baltimore. (EPFL)

Compromise was not working. It could not work as the hundreds of Southern volunteers crowded into the Norfolk-bound steamers in the early months of 1861, saluting passing ships, one or two of which flew the pennant of "The Republic of South Carolina."

The new wave was one of vengeance, of dedication, of Harriet Beecher Stowe, who, when Virginia finally seceded and the Baltimore riots began, exulted that a "cause to die for" had finally arrived.

"We wake to the higher aims of a land that has lost for a little her love of gold, her love of a peace that was full of wrongs and shames," said the small but mighty northern author of "Uncle Tom's Cabin."

Far to the south of her, Maryland was beginning her great ordeal. When it was over, the state would have little but a bad name, a fine anthem, a tragic legend and thousands of dead sons.

In February of 1861, warned by Philadelphia railroad men and by detective Allan Pinkerton of a "Baltimore plot" on his life, Abraham Lincoln agreed somewhat reluctantly to a furtive and unscheduled trip through Baltimore on the way to his inauguration. The "plot" has remained forever shadowy and Pinkerton's part in it somewhat overdrawn, but the ruse disgusted Maryland editors and added fuel to pro-Southern fury in Eastern parts of the state.

Tumultuous, fast-moving events added fuel to the flame—Fort Sumter on April 12 and a Federal call for Union volunteers (not answered, so far as is known, by a single Baltimore citizen).

The path to violence

On April 18, Pennsylvanians moving south through Baltimore from Bolton station were hissed and bombarded with bricks.

The next day a 35-car trainload of troops, the Sixth Massachusetts regiment, arrived at the President Street station at the eastern end of town.

A sheet music depiction of the Maryland Guard in Zouave uniforms popularized by the French. These men are believed to have sailed away for the C. S. A. (EPFL)

Crowds await the arrival of the President-elect. They were disappointed. (EPFL)

They were armed, but somehow, instead of forming to march to Camden Station, one mile west, were kept in their cars for a horsedrawn trip along rails, the conventional route for civilians. A few cars got through, scarred with a fusillade of stones and shattered windows.

Fighting begins in earnest

About one third of the way along their path, derisive, disorderly crowds blocked the car route with sand, anchors and stones pulled off the docks near Gay and Pratt streets. They showered the troop cars with paving stones.

Then the troops reformed on foot for the march to Camden station, about 30 blocks away.

Their route was bedlam. At every block on the east side stones were hurled and the angry crowd turned into a mob of pistol-wielding insurgents.

The New Englanders fired a volley and then another and the line of march became a running fight between citizens and soldiers.

The New Englanders crossed this bridge, going west into the full fury of the riot. (EPFL)

A doorway in the 300 block of East Pratt street where one citizen fell, a casualty of the uproar. (EPFL)

Camden Station, a mid-Victorian idea of a reproduction of Independence Hall, where the Sixth Massachusetts was headed. Some of them didn't make it. (EPFL)

Along East Pratt street. (LC)

The battered Sixth Massachusetts encampment at Relay on the way to Washington. (LC)

The riot toll mounts

Baltimore's mayor, mild-spirited George William Brown, rushed from Camden Station, to help quell the trouble along Pratt street, but things were too far gone. Citizens, soldiers were falling on both sides. They were dragged into storefronts for emergency care or rescued from the mob by fellow soldiers.

Somehow, most of the sorely tried regiment made it to Camden station and boarded for Washington, shooting an innocent citizen who happened to cheer for Jefferson Davis as he stood along the B&O line southward.

Four soldiers and dozens of private citizens had been killed and injured.

Luther Ladd, a fatality in the ranks of the Sixth Massachusetts. (EPFL)

George William Brown, armed only with an umbrella, failed to quiet the rioters. (BS)

A crowd gathers at a Baltimore bookstore, waiting for news of riot aftermath. (EPFL)

Euphoria and anarchy

Maryland leaders pled with Lincoln and the military to route all forthcoming troop movements around Baltimore, and for a time the government did so.

Baltimore tottered on the brink of independence under a flag of anarchy and orders went out to burn the bridges to the north of the city and prevent any more Pratt streets.

Some observers took the fight as a cue that Maryland would secede. In far-off Louisiana, James Ryder Randall wrote the words to "Maryland, My Maryland", a stirring hymn welcoming his home state to the Confederacy. Hetty and Jenny Cary, attractive and fashionable residents of the city's Mount Vernon district, took the words, matched them to the song and took both to the camps of the Confederate army a few months later.

Reprisals and a firm, federal hand

It could not last. On May 5, General Ben Butler, popular Massachusetts leader and Democratic big shot, seized the important rail junction at Relay house, just south of Baltimore.

On May 13 he occupied strategic Federal Hill which still faces the main commercial heart of the state.

Marylanders did not know it yet, but the state was secured for the Union. Federal troops did not neglect Fort McHenry, which they immediately stocked with mountains of small arms seized from Baltimore city for the defense of the metropolis.

James Ryder Randall. (EPFL)

Hetty Cary. (MHS)

Ready for action, troops of General Nathaniel Banks take over the basement of the Customs Building. (EPFL)

With Maryland apparently secure, Duryea's Zouaves took up this encampment overlooking city harbor. (EPFL)

Somerset county Union loyalist, Anna Ella Carroll, (1815-1894), freed her slaves as the war started, gave valued counsel to Lincoln. Her remedy for rebellion; seize the Tennessee River valley and split the South, a plan adopted in 1862. (MHS)

The Twelfth New York, on the alert at Annapolis and en route to Washington. (LC)

Downtown Baltimore would have been in a bad way if the Federal Hill gun in the foreground had cut loose in May, 1861. (EPFL)

A Harper's Weekly artist caught rebel prisoners leaving for Fortress Monroe, Va., in 1861 (LC)

Constitutional crisis

In the roundup of Southern sympathizers and suspects, the Federals bagged John Merryman who had burned a bridge in the effort to protect Baltimore on April 20.

Locked up in Fort McHenry without charges, he was claimed before Chief Justice Taney under a move by his lawyers. When the writ of *habeas corpus* was refused, Taney issued the famous opinion of *Ex Parte Merryman*. It says that no President can suspend the writ of *habeas corpus*, as had happened to Merryman. It also adds that military officers cannot prosecute citizens otherwise subject to the courts and laws of the United States.

A calmer city

By mid-summer, calm at gunpoint had settled over the city. To the South, train traffic resumed and some troops were even moved through town. Signs of Union loyalty blossomed, although there was sometimes a cannon just up the street. Most important to Lincoln, the lines to the South and West were safe.

Keeping the line open

Lumber for hospitals and barracks, stoves, clothes, coal and food had to move to an isolated Washington as the war fury mounted.

Railroads were the answer and Lincoln leaned heavily on the services of B&O president John Work Garrett. A direct telegraph line was soon set up linking Mount Clare headquarters of the road with the War Department.

Over this line, and the ones to the west poured countless messages of troop movements, confederate raids and troop movements. Hundreds of bridges were burned, some many times, and a vast store of bent rails and shattered engines accumulated in Eastern Maryland to be melted down into rails to be relaid.

Roger Brooke Taney. (EPFL)

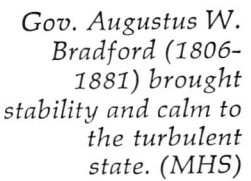

Gov. Augustus W. Bradford (1806-1881) brought stability and calm to the turbulent state. (MHS)

John W. Garrett, (1820-1884) was a tower of strength. (BS)

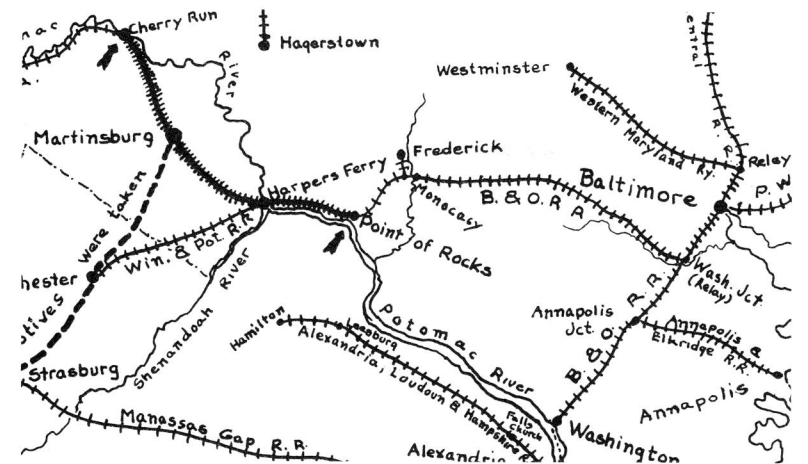

The war arena, partly a patchwork of local lines, with the B&O straddling the center. Map by L. W. Sagle of the main Confederate targets of the war. (BORRM)

Baltimore and Ohio Railroad
TELEGRAM,
From Wash'n July 5 1864
Received, Baltimore, 7 o'clock, 50 min. P.M.
To J W Garrett
You say telegraphic communication is re-established with Sandy Hook. Well what does Sandy Hook say about operation of enemy & of Sigel doing today
A. Lincoln

Baltimore and Ohio Railroad
TELEGRAM,
From Wash July 9th 1864
Received, Baltimore, 5 o'clock, 21 min. P.M.
To J W Garrett Prest
What have you heard about a battle at Monocacy today. We have nothing about it here except what you say
A Lincoln

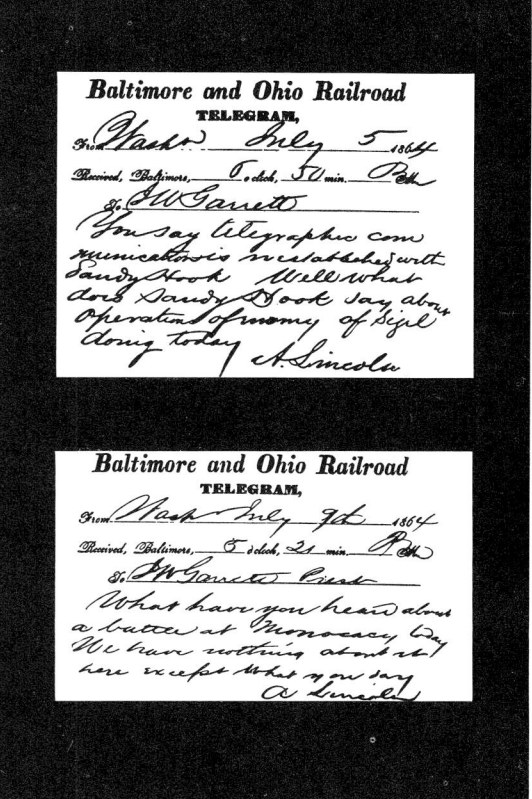

Lincoln asks Garrett for news of a battle on the Monocacy, July 1864. (BORRM)

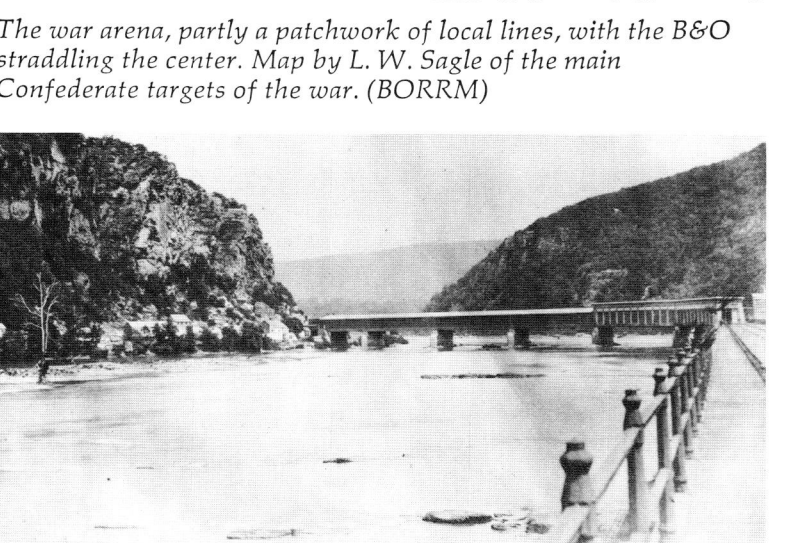

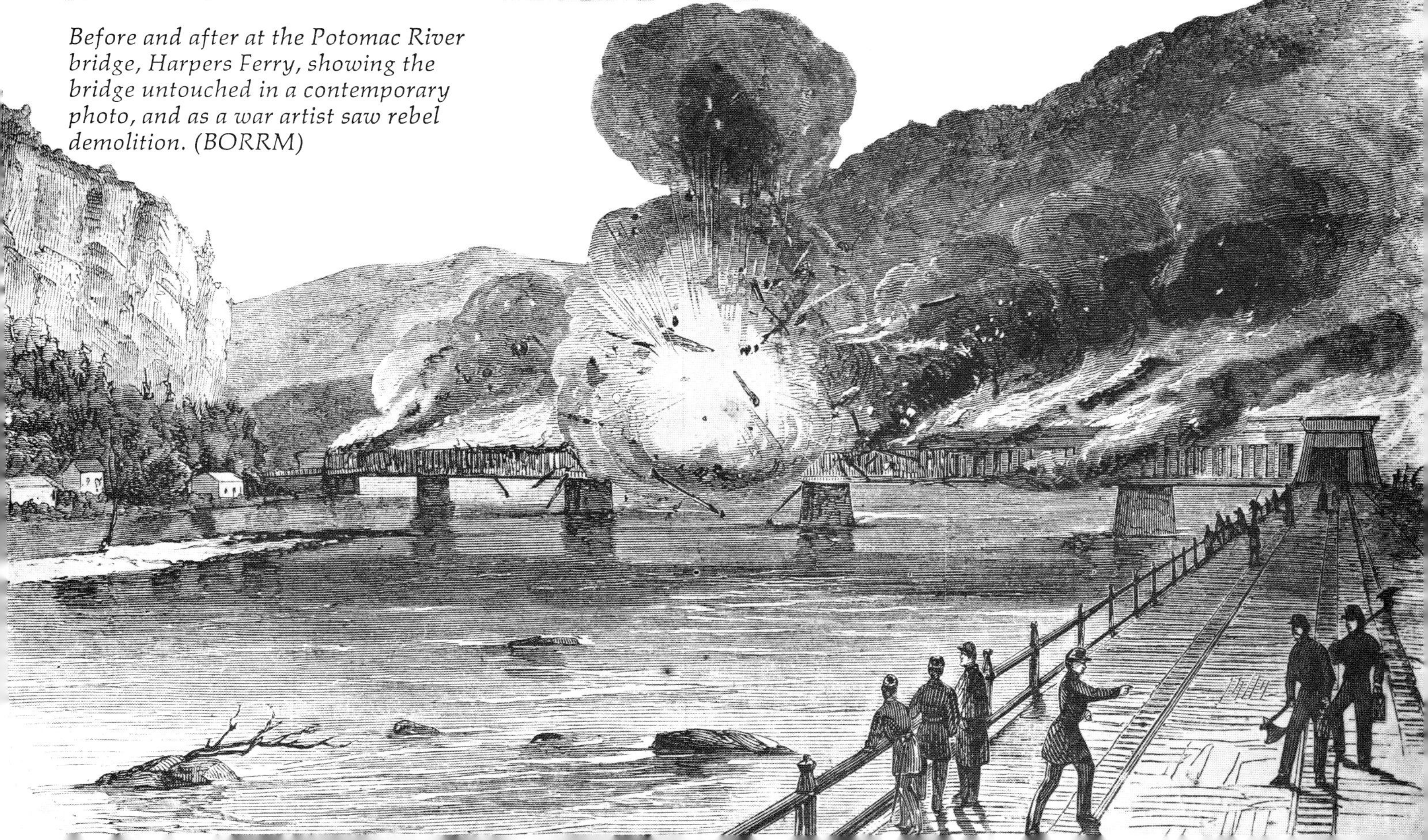

Before and after at the Potomac River bridge, Harpers Ferry, showing the bridge untouched in a contemporary photo, and as a war artist saw rebel demolition. (BORRM)

Patchwork and profits

From mid-1861 until the summer of the next year, the main stem of the B&O to Wheeling, W. Va. was virtually inoperable, thanks to Confederate raids and sabotage.

More than 125 bridges were destroyed, and repaired, often within a few days.

Despite the terrific destruction, the heaviest industrial damage up to that date suffered anywhere, the railroad managed to show a $2 million profit for fiscal 1861.

An Antietam portfolio . . .

Robert E. Lee moved against Maryland in force in early September, 1862 and by September 6 he had reached Frederick, where a legend was born.

Barbara Freitchie, an aged resident of 96, is supposed to have defied the rebels by flying a Union flag from her window and shouting her loyalty to none other than Stonewall Jackson—a legend that may never have happened that way, but one which stirred the North mightily in John Greenleaf Whittier's famous poem.

Legends were not on Lee's mind, and he soon sent Stonewall westward to cover his rear by taking Harpers Ferry, an event achieved in about a half hour with the help of a massive shelling by Maryland's Confederate artillery.

A prelude at South Mountain

With his army split in two, Lee moved to safer quarters west, behind South Mountain. By this time Union forces, who had captured Lee's battle plan wrapped up along with three cigars dropped by a staff officer, were well informed and moving.

They fell on the Confederates just east of South Mountain, driving them back further westward toward Hagerstown.

Cautiously, Lee took up a position just west of Sharpsburg, a village between Antietam creek and the Potomac. McClellan's Union forces were swelled by huge levies racing across Maryland. About 30,000 arrived within three days.

A fanciful version of the Barbara Freitchie affair. Stonewall stayed away. (LC)

A locomotive burned by Stonewall Jackson's men, out of action at Martinsburg, W. Va. (BORRM)

Heading out of Boonsboro, Union troops of General Joseph Hooker splash through the upper Antietam creek on their way to the Hagerstown pike the day before the great battle (EPFL)

Feeling out the enemy

Scouts, artillery duellists and signalmen, crowding the mountain tops of the rugged area, tested the strength of both armies while the Union lines formed just east of Sharpsburg, spanning the Boonsboro road and Antietam creek.

The fight opened on the morning of September 17. The Union attack was composed of three furious slashes against Lee's left, center and right, in that order. Objects of the assault were the Hagerstown road and Dunker church, on the north, the "sunken road" which linked the pike with the Boonsboro road in the middle of the line and on the south the lower Antietam bridge, forever linked to the name of Ambrose Burnside.

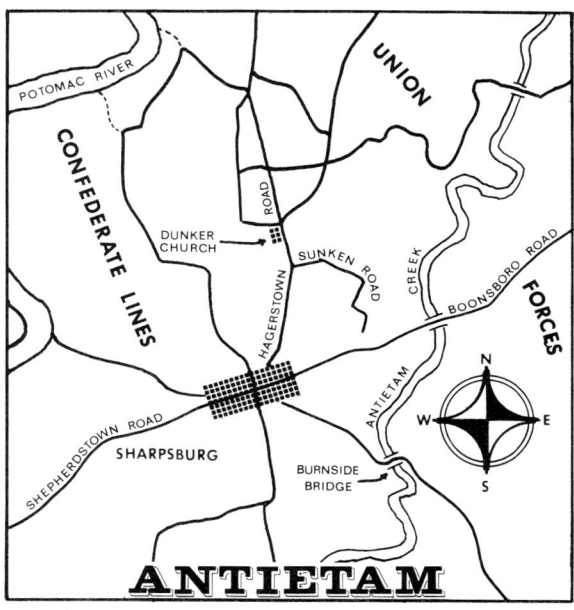

A map of the area of the struggle. (KM)

A Union scout looks for the enemy with field glasses. (EPFL)

Famed cameraman Timothy O'Sullivan caught these Union signalmen searching for the Confederate artillery on Elk mountain near Antietam. (LC)

A. P. Hill to the rescue

Rebel artillery and sharpshooters were dug in southeast of the city, taking a terrible toll of Northern troops as General Burnside tried again and again to cross Antietam via the bridge.

To the north, New York's Irish brigade met a horrific defense on the sunken road and nearby, battle see-sawed around Dunker church and through the "east" and "west" woods on both sides of the Hagerstown road.

By about 4 P. M., Burnside, with the help of Maryland Union troops, finally made it across the bridge and Lee was in peril, or would have been.

Harpers Ferry reinforcements under Gen. A. P. Hill of the C. S. A. arrived within minutes and launched an overwhelming counter attack.

Burnside's charges finally cross the bridge after great slaughter. They could have waded across, say military experts. (MHS)

Theatrical, but accurate to the last detail was a 1962 enactment of Antietam, photographed by A. Aubrey Bodine. (AAB)

A barn is pressed into service as a Union hospital. (LC)

Supply trains to support Union General Burnside are shown passing Antietam Iron works, well shot up. (EPFL)

Terrified civilians took shelter in the aptly-named "Killing's Cave." (MHS)

End of a stalemate

By nightfall, both armies were exhausted, though both held firm positions at the end of the day. The Northern army, which had come close to victory, would not commit its last reserves. The next evening the Confederates forded the river near Shepherdstown and moved into the safety of Virginia.

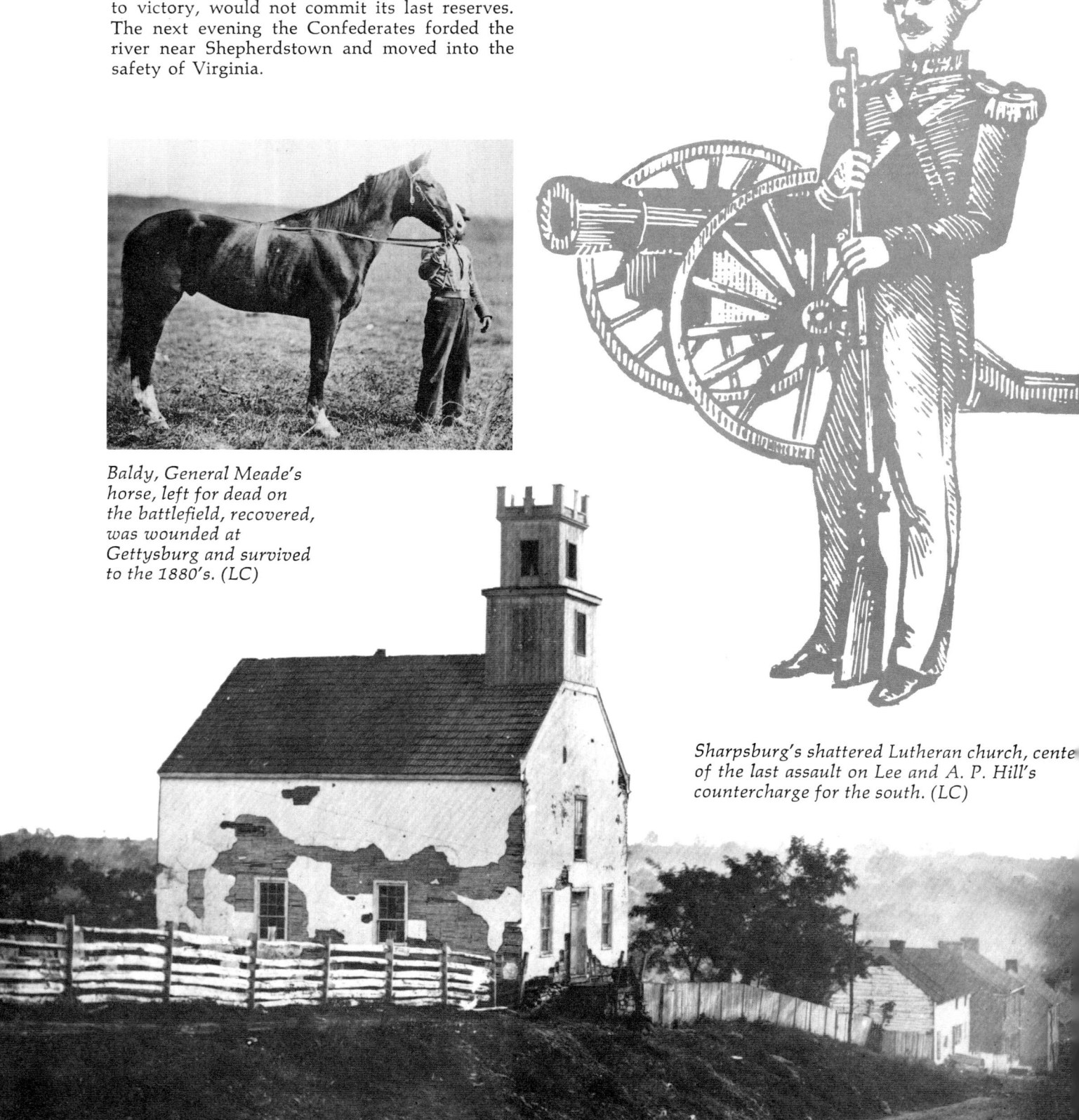

Baldy, General Meade's horse, left for dead on the battlefield, recovered, was wounded at Gettysburg and survived to the 1880's. (LC)

Sharpsburg's shattered Lutheran church, center of the last assault on Lee and A. P. Hill's countercharge for the south. (LC)

The slaughter at the "rail fence" on the Hagerstown pike. (LC)

The dead ring Dunker church. (LC)

Indiana volunteers caring for the wounded in makeshift hospital tents. (LC)

Marylanders who wore the blue and the gray . . .

A Baltimore attorney, Maj. Gen. John Reese Kenly (1822-1891) was a major defense commander for Maryland, refused a Federal pension for his services. (MHS)

Cumberland-born Otho Cresap Ord (1818-1883) rose to major general's rank, a West Pointer who stayed with the Union. He saw wide service in the west and the closing battles around Richmond. (MHS)

Rear Admiral Louis M. Goldsborough, (1805-1877) served in the Mexican War, played a leading role in the capture of Roanoke Island for the Union. (MHS)

Conscience-stricken Franklin Buchanan (1800–1864) was first superintendent of the Naval Academy but joined the Confederate Navy. Wounded twice, he loomed large in the defense of Mobile bay and the ironclad attack by the Virginia in Hampton Roads. (EPFL)

Rear Admiral Raphael Semmes (1809-1877) was a Charles countian who sank 82 Union ships as a Confederate raider, lost the Alabama off Cherbourg, France. (EPFL)

Bradley T. Johnson (1829–1903) of Frederick, was a Confederate brigadier of dashing mien. His call for an uprising in Maryland before Antietam was fierier than that of Robert E. Lee. Few responded. (MHS)

Brig. Gen. Lloyd Tilghman, (1816-1863) of Talbot county, bore two of the Eastern Shore's oldest names. A former railroad engineer, he figured in the western campaign and died for the South at Baker's Hill in 1863. (LC)

The bloodiest day . . .

Nothing like Antietam, for sheer carnage, had been seen so far in the war and the brutal cost revolted northerners and southerners alike. There were about 22,000 casualties and about 6,000 killed within the space of 8 or 9 hours.

The truth was, that Antietam marked the first moment when two veteran armies clashed. Earlier engagements had featured raw levies, whose sheer footpower to the rear could protect them.

As the bloodiest single day in the American Civil War, the terrible scene of Antietam can be mentioned only with Shiloh, Cold Harbor, Gettysburg and Fredericksburg.

Tactically, it settled little, except the fate of union commander George Brinton McClellan. He was fired.

After Antietam, Hagerstown ladies deliver food to the wounded in Union hospitals. (EPFL)

Capt. William H. Murray, left and Pvt. Caphan Murray pose in the uniform of the Maryland Fifth regiment. The captain was wounded at Gettysburg. (EPFL)

A wagon train crosses the Burnside bridge after the battle. (LC)

Beleagured Baltimore

Military rule settled over Baltimore as the war wore on and the police power became a virtual function of the federal military. In the mills and armories of the Patapsco, however, the city became an arsenal, crowded with shipping and churning out vessels of war, crates of hardtack, flags, cloth and canvas.

At 66 South Sharp street, Mrs. Catherine Sumwalt stitched away busily on a new dress for Mary Todd Lincoln and on July 3 of 1862, Mrs. Lincoln sent one of her pets, John E. Wool, the Fort McHenry commander, a bouquet of flowers.

The theaters were packed, the saloons likewise and trade all over the Bay began to revive at mid-point in the conflict.

Black leaders, with the help of Maryland attorneys, won full play for black soldiers in the pay line, reversing government order. (LC)

Humble hardtack, a flour and water biscuit, was shipped by the ton from Baltimore bakeries. It was fried, toasted, dunked, crumbled up in soups and coffee and occasionally digested. (AC)

Baltimore harbor, crowded with ships and goods late in the war. (WC)

Melodrama queen Adah Isaacs Menken, (1835-1868), hung a portrait of Robert E. Lee in her theater dressing room. Police took her into custody. (LC)

A sobering spirit

As the Confederate flags were packed away in attics, Baltimore's tone changed and the city and state began to genuinely fear invasion—from the South.

Civil War drills and meetings often centered at Guy's Monument house, downtown Baltimore hostelry. (EPFL)

Constant alarms from Confederate cavalry kept Baltimore under siege. This barricade went up in 1863 at West Saratoga and Pine streets. (EPFL)

The *Three Brothers,* a vessel launched in 1857, was converted into a ram to go after Confederate ironclads. (EPFL)

The conservative, but loyal Union party, founded in Baltimore in 1860, meets in the First Presbyterian church, 1864. (LC)

The high tide sweeps north

Nothing could quiet the state permanently as long as the swift, massive Army of Northern Virginia still had fight. It swept north in June of 1863 and for most of Maryland the great battle ahead was a case of watching and waiting for the Confederate scouts, of nursing tremendous casualties from both armies who swamped the barns, barracks, churches and homes of the piedmont and its towns.

The assembly of soldiers at Gettysburg drew thousands of relatives of those engaged who swarmed over every railroad in the east, bound for the battle.

Marylanders fought Marylanders at Culp's Hill, Gettysburg. (MHS)

Hanover Junction, Pa., terminus of the Gettysburg line. (LC)

Meade's leisurely pursuit of the vanishing rebels, shown here at Brunswick, angered war hawks and the cabinet. (LC)

Confederate cavalry ransacks New Windsor in 1863 invasion. (MHS)

The last alarm

It was again mid-summer, this time 1864, and the hazard of war again swept through Maryland, this time the huge thrust of General Jubal Early that opened on July 6.

Vengeful southern troops raided Williamsport, Boonsboro, Sharpsburg and other smaller centers, looting the countryside of property.

At the Battle of the Monocacy southeast of Frederick a weak Federal force under General Lew Wallace slowed the Early advance long enough to bring up major resistance from Washington.

A plot to seize the huge Confederate prison camp at Point Lookout and arm 17,000 rebels with weapons from the North, misfired.

Washington, and Baltimore, never the target of the rebels strategically, were safe.

Maryland raider Harry Gilmor scattered Union forces at lightly defended points, terrified Towson, Timonium, Cockeysville and Kingsville. (LC)

Mosby's "partisans", including many Maryland rebels, in a moment of rest. (MHS)

Eastern Shore artist Allen C. Redwood, Confederate prisoner, painted this baptism scene at Fort Delaware, favorite lockup for Maryland officers of the C. S. A. (MHS)

Maryland raiders faced the Third Massachusetts in trim encampment at Fort Lincoln. (LC)

The final tragedy

All but slaveholders, who were ruined by the precipitate drop in prices, gained in enthusiasm as the long and bloody encounter finally showed signs of ending.

Arrivals included the prisoners and the slaves freed.

In dark, gaslit rooms in the "wrong" sections of Baltimore and Washington, half-drunken conspirators plotted the final act.

Four hundred days in Confederate prisons, including Andersonville, left these men of the Ninth Maryland regiment, U. S. A., undaunted and somehow, with a drum. (EPFL)

Freedmen arrive in Baltimore as the great conflict ends. (LC)

Summoning Samuel Arnold by telegram to a secret conference at Barnum's City hotel, Baltimore, John Wilkes Booth, (1838-1865), began the final, fatal phase of his Lincoln plot. (EPFL)

Samuel Arnold, of Hookstown, got cold feet at the last minute, told Booth "I have ceased with you" and stayed away from the murder scene. (LC)

John Wilkes Booth (EPFL)

The Booth reward poster. (EPFL)

Reverdy Johnson, dean of the Maryland bar, defended the Lincoln conspirators, then quit when the trial became what he thought was a legal lynching. (BS)

While Lincoln's body lay in state in the rotunda of Latrobe's exchange, Mary Todd Lincoln had a brief collation at Eutaw House. (MHS)

Tudor Hall, home of John Wilkes and family, near Bel Air. (EPFL)

Bryantown tavern in southern Maryland, where Booth stopped on his escape. (EPFL)

With the war over, Zouaves of the Union Army parade down Broadway, East Baltimore. (EPFL)

More than 62,000 Marylanders were in the Union's armed forces and about 22,000 in the ranks of the South. One of them was Joshua Riggs. (EPFL)

1865 1918
THE BANNERED YEARS

THE GREAT, GOLDEN years between the Civil War and the armistice of 1918 seemed to prosperous Americans of that time like a long holiday, broken only by two short wars that left the country's resources and spirits untouched.

These were the "good old days" of sentimental memory—two full generations of rising hopes for the middle class, unheard of luxuries for the rich.

Life indeed could be pleasant when oysters were something like a penny a piece. Whatever else they were, the vanished Victorian-Edwardian generation gave every evidence of having a good time, based on the glowing photographic remains of the age.

Things still moved slowly in Nineteenth Century America. Government, despite the bluster of politicians, took on a low-keyed, parochial tone tied to minimizing revenues. No matter how much this might have pleased Thomas Jefferson, the era soon proved inadequate in leadership and in the public funding of the sort that can cope with problems in an industrial age.

For the first four decades of the post Civil War period, Maryland affairs were pretty consistently dominated by politicoes like U. S. Senator Arthur Pue Gorman, whose death-grip on the Maryland General Assembly assured him of a high place in national Democratic councils, and of his ally, Eastern Shoreman I. Freeman Rasin, who became a Baltimore political boss.

Black suffrage created a new Republican-oriented voting block in Southern Maryland counties, but it was not powerful enough to stop regressive moves against blacks, including a disgraceful attempt, actually passed by the General Assembly, to take voting rights away from them through a literacy test gimmick.

On the plus side, the state made strides in pulling together its patchwork of public school education, and the new Constitution of 1864 looked toward uniformity in county public education. By the late 1860's, Maryland had 71,000 children enrolled in a more or less standardized system of education.

A group reading the Aberdeen Enterprise *and the auction notices outside the newspaper offices about 1890. The typesetter smoked a pipe. (ML)*

Progress in public health was slower. As late as 1900, Baltimore had no general public sanitary sewer system—a gleeful discovery for budding journalist, Henry L. Mencken who conducted a world series of metropolitan disease, a box score tally in which Baltimore publicly swamped the city of Constantinople. Commercial prosperity returned to the Bay region a few years after the war. It at least doubled the ranks of the affluent. The new timber and coal barons, the bankers of that age, built themselves 15, 20 and even 30-room mansions to herald their arrival.

Late in the Victorian period, Hagerstown emerged as a new industrial and distribution center, outstripping Frederick and approaching Cumberland in population and activity. Baltimore regained the lost southern distribution and manufacturing trade and enlarged it, but lost out to New York city as a world port, partly because of an insistence on the use of coastal sailers and steamers, rather than global packets, operating between world trade centers.

This was, nevertheless, the heyday of the Bay steamboat, white and gaudily gilded sidewheelers and stern-powered ships that brought product and visitors and romance to docks all over the Delmarva tidewater.

The vast communication expanse brought the telephone and the telegraph to full flower and the transcontinental luxury train, as well as the first nibbles at the auto age. At College Park, educators laid the nucleus for what was to become one of the nation's paramount agricultural research centers. The wealth of Nineteenth Century mercantile fortunes was showered on Baltimore in the form of new aids to art and education.

Nothing added more to everyday pleasure for the Victorians, and possibly to us in appreciating their life, than the development of relatively cheap camera equipment and printing techniques. This was the first era in history that was charted by amateur artists ranging up into the millions. It was also recorded by professionals in a mammoth output of stereo slides, *carte de visite* portraits and later by the simple snapshot and by billions of postcards.

Much of it reflects everyday events in a tranquil age and in Maryland the trend was highlighted by such major technicians as Elias M. Recher of Frederick and W. J. Chase, of Baltimore.

They wrote the visual record and it is a vivacious one.

Gearing up for education and agriculture

Education would solve the world's ills, or so believed the uplift set in the late Nineteenth Century. They set out to prove it with advances in agricultural methods and training and a broad approach to popular education including World's Fairs and specialized institutions for the afflicted.

Help for the deaf began in a major way in 1866 with building of the main hall for the Maryland School for the Deaf, Frederick, a Victorian fantasy razed in 1967. (ML)

Enjoying the air

It was "Meet me in St. Louie, Louis" in 1904 when the world's fair opened. The two attendants in the Maryland agricultural exhibit, surrounded by tobacco leaf, canned oysters and agricultural products were waiting for crowds to appear. (ML)

Where they stayed and played in the seventies

Marylanders relaxed after the guns were racked up at Appomattox. Here are some of the resorts from the era of General Grant.

Rail lines led directly to the Western Maryland resorts like the Deer Park hotel, Garrett county. (EPFL)

The Albion, a still-standing boarding hotel in Baltimore's Mount Vernon district. (EPFL)

The Pen Mar station near the summit in well-painted glory. (WC)

A leisurely view of Cumberland Narrows, where Washington went west. (WC)

Vacationers on an outing in the rocks at Blue Ridge Summit. (WC)

A Guerilla war on the Chesapeake

Illegal moonlight oyster dredgers from Virginia and the back coves of the Bay were ruining the Maryland beds throughout the 1880's. Pirate activity had dropped production to 10 million bushels a year. Maryland mounted an official "navy," armed with 6-pounders, Naval Academy cannon, to chase the raiders. The "oyster war" became a national cause. Here is one scene from the chase.

The monument mania

No one dared deny monuments to the eager audience—the ceremony-hungry crowds of the gilded age. Here are four samples from the past. The Emerson Tower was raised by Capt. Isaac Emerson, developer of Bromo Seltzer, and it was built complete with a bottle of the product in downtown Baltimore. Gapland is a 50-foot masonry arch dedicated to Civil War correspondents and was finished under the leadership of Eastern Shoreman George A. Townsend (1841-1914) on South Mountain. Dedication of the Maryland line monument in Baltimore's Mount Royal district is shown. Heroic Antietam soldier's memorial is shown ready for shipment in a Rhode Island studio. That's General Tom Thumb, of P. T. Barnum fame, and wife at the lower left.

A two-boat encounter off Swann point. (EPFL)

Maryland Line memorial (EPFL)

Gapland (EPFL)

Tom Thumb and friends (WC)

Emerson's tower (EPFL)

Riding the line with Dan Willard

From the 1890's and forward, Maryland trains were setting the national pace for luxury and service, no small tribute to Daniel Willard, autocratic, no-nonsense boss of the B&O.

Daniel Willard (EPFL)

Electric engines arrived in 1895, a pioneering anti-pollution effort designed to keep smoke out of the Baltimore tunnels. (BORRM)

Lamps hissed and coffee steamed as a railroad crew listened while a guitarist performed, "There's a little box of pine on the 7:09," famous tear jerker of the era. (BORRM)

Four magnificent gestures to the future

No American city has been equally favored with this quartet of personal bequests, rooted in Nineteenth Century fortunes made in international trade, railroading and manufacturing, but given freely to Maryland culture and the future of the world.

A posthumous gift of $7 million, largest private philanthropy in American history up to that time by Johns Hopkins (1795–1873), revolutionized American graduate school training and founded a great hospital. (EPFL)

George Peabody, Massachusetts-born financier, dedicated the Peabody Institute in 1866 and is the founding father of Maryland institutional culture in music and art training. (EPFL)

Enoch Pratt founded the public library system of Baltimore city, open to "all citizens regardless of property or color," a system that has since become a model and inspired the later benefactions of Andrew Carnegie. (EPFL)

Henry Walters presented his princely collection of traditional art from all epochs to the city of Baltimore and world scholarship, a gesture equalled by only a handful of Americans including Isabella Gardner of Boston and William Rockhill Nelson, of Kansas City. (WAG)

Reflections grave and gay

Theatre life, parades and a few disasters marked Maryland life in the last quarter of the Nineteenth Century.

Worst Maryland civilian disaster of the age — 63 persons drowning at the Tivoli picnic grounds when a pier collapsed in 1883. (EPFL)

A resolute attempt to throw the rascals out and Horace Greeley in, at Ford's opera house, 1872. (LC)

The legendary Oriole baseball team of 1894–1896, which won three consecutive world championships. (BS)

What the well-dressed postman wore at the turn of the century. (EPFL)

Dandies of Maryland's 5th regiment all dolled up at Long Branch, Frederick county, 1874. (EPFL)

Cutting capers at a Dandy Fifth encampment in 1886 at Atlantic City. (EPFL)

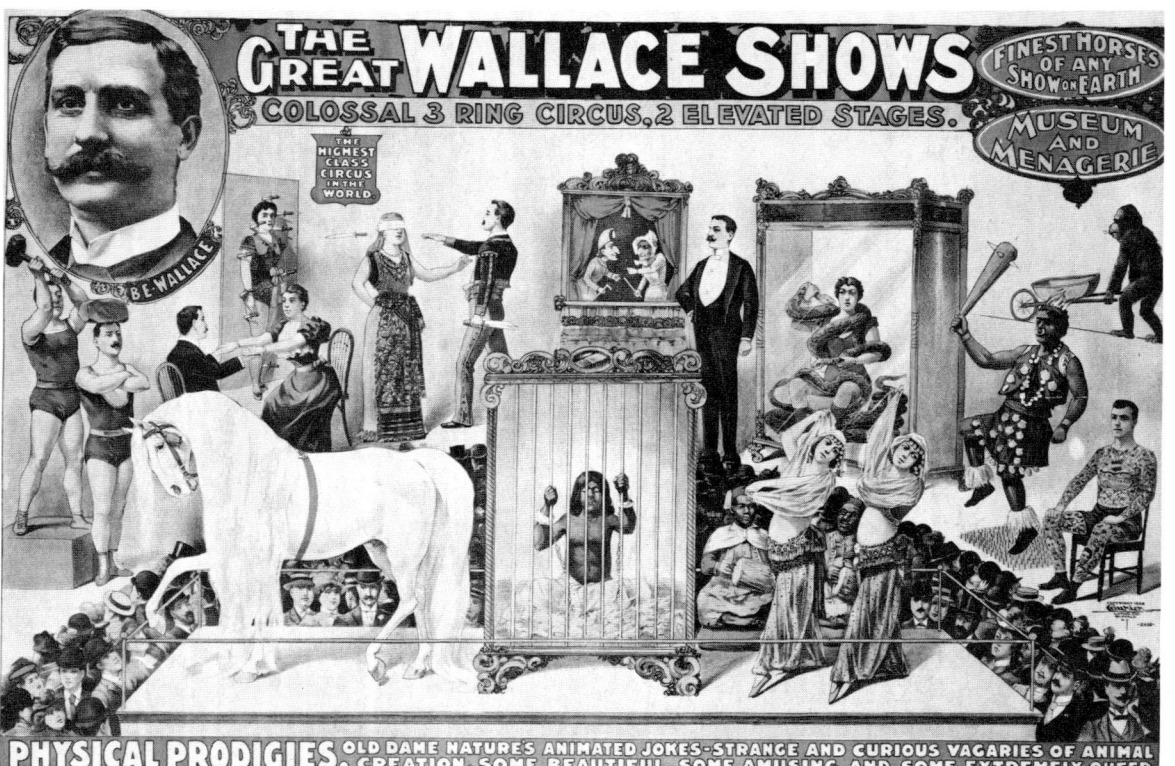

A show-stopping circus of 1898. (LC)

Blacks voted for the first time in 1870 and here emancipation is being celebrated in Mount Vernon square, Baltimore. (LC)

John T. Ford's theater empire on the Chesapeake in poster form. (LC)

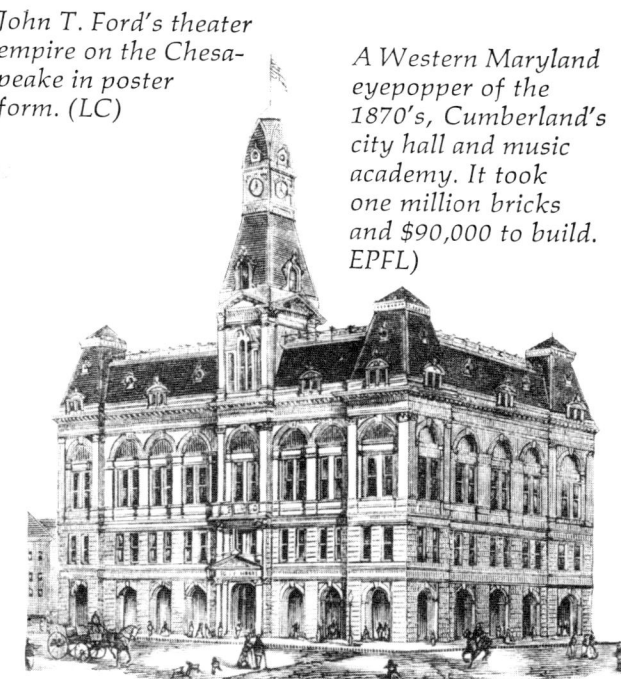

A Western Maryland eyepopper of the 1870's, Cumberland's city hall and music academy. It took one million bricks and $90,000 to build. EPFL)

The workaday world, a Baltimore county blacksmith's shop about 1870. (WC)

Dreamy college days

By the 1890's, Maryland colleges and graduate schools were graduating masses of specially trained students, but all was not labor as one of these campus scenes shows.

A University hospital operating theater about 1895. (ML)

The College Park football 16 (with coach?) of 1893–1894. (ML)

Some local disasters

Firebells rang, little boys ran and strong men coped when these local sensations burst upon an unwary world.

A highwire act was in order for C&P repairmen in 1914 after a seven-ton truck, loaded with sand, went into the pole. Clifton Park is on the left. (CPM)

Raising a pole after a 1902 tornado de-roofed a church and, nearby, Evering's saloon at East Eager and McDonogh streets, Baltimore. (EPFL)

A damp dip for harbor police followed a plunge of a trolley car off a Baltimore bridge in 1913. (EPFL)

One solution to the traffic problem along Baltimore's Charles street in the 1890's. (EPFL)

Maryland's College Park campus was devastated in November, 1912 when the old main building burned. (ML)

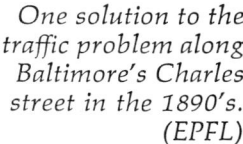

It was 1910 along Race street, Cambridge and the town turned out to view the remains of the Methodist church. (EPFL)

A student of the English heroine, Florence Nightingale, Miss Louise Parsons founded the Johns Hopkins nursing school, was first superintendent of medical training for the University of Maryland. (ML)

Women to the fore

The post-Civil War Maryland woman was liberated by contrast to her crinoline counterpart. She entered the professions and spoke out on public issues, though not yet a voter, and she invaded higher education in force.

Dr. Florence Rena Sabin became the first woman professor in a medical school and Frances Ellen Watkins Harper, the first black woman poet of note, first publishing in 1854.

Frances E. Willard, patron saint of Prohibition, surrounded by ladies of the Women's Christian Temperance Union at a Maryland convention in the 1890's. (EPFL)

Miss Mamie Phipps, a telephone operator and Salisbury fashion queen in turn of the century dress. (CPM)

Lady cyclists on an outing to Penwood Park in 1897. (EPFL)

Homes of the hardly poor

If you were rich in the high Victorian period and had $50,000 to $250,000 in cash to spend you did this and you wanted acres of turkey carpet, portieres, black walnut woodwork, stained glass and 8 maids who would work for $8 a week. Of these marvelous specimens of fun architecture, only a few, including Cylburn, survive.

Castellated splendor was the order of the day at the Jacob Tome house, Port Deposit. (EPFL)

The 27-room "Fair Meadows" at Harford Furnace was built of Port Deposit granite by Clement Dietrich in 1871. (EPFL)

Finest of all the Italianate mansions, but not the largest, was Richard Upjohn's Wyman Villa. (EPFL)

Not an awning was wrinkled at manicured "Cylburn" a North Baltimore extravaganza. Queen Victoria would have loved it. (EPFL)

The ladies console a Spanish-American War encampment, probably at Pimlico, in 1898. (EPFL)

Time out for a quickie war

American troops and sailors crumpled the Spanish Empire in a short, glorious 1898 encounter. The heroes were home almost before the guns cooled, but disease took many lives.

A trio of Maryland war troopers, one, at left, complete with monocle. (EPFL)

Hysteria swept Maryland after Admiral Dewey blasted the Spanish squadron out of Manila Bay without the loss of a single man. The Olympia led the van, closely followed by the cruiser Baltimore. *(LC)*

Arthur Pue Gorman (EPFL)

Politicoes and patricians

These Maryland men were much in the public eye as 1890 rolled around. Senator Arthur Pue Gorman still held power but bore the scars of epochal encounters with reformers, including Charles Joseph Bonaparte, a crony of Theodore Roosevelt. He went on to play a leading national role in the "trust busting" of the early 1900's.

Popular Howard county farmer and editor Edwin Warfield, the very picture of a Colonel Sanders patrician, was an easy winner in the 1903 gubernatorial race.

Charles Bonaparte (EPFL)

Gov. Warfield and party thrill Bel Air spectators in 1905. (ML)

Sensing a victory, the Democratic party gathers in the scorching Baltimore heat of July, 1912, nominating Woodrow Wilson, after William Jennings Bryan swung his support to the New Jersey Governor. (BNA)

Handsome Frank Brown, Baltimore postmaster, sits beside his 1887 Christmas present, a rendering of his post office in flowers. He was Maryland's governor from 1892 to 1896. (EPFL)

Hagerstown's William T. Hamilton was Gorman's first sponsor and was Maryland governor in the early 1880's.

An acquaintance of Lafayette when a teenager, Robert Milligan McLane (1815–1898), served the nation brilliantly as French ambassador in the turbulent 1880's. (EPFL)

A foursome for mankind

In the later Victorian age, nowhere in the world was there a more lauded group than the "Big Four" of Johns Hopkins medicine.

Dr. William H. Welch (1850–1934), a Connecticut native, selected the original hospital staff and was a master pathologist and bacteriologist. (EPFL)

Sir William Osler (1849–1919), a Canadian, was the hospital's first physician in chief and later moved to Oxford where he was knighted by George V. (EPFL)

Dr. William Stewart Halsted (1852–1922), first professor of surgery for the Hopkins, was a New York city native, founded the school of surgery, probably first in the field using scientific method. (JHH)

Dr. Howard A. Kelly (1858–1943), was a Philadelphian, outstanding surgeon and world authority on gynecology. (EPFL)

The auto age arrives

Marylanders began their romance with the automobile three generations ago. Here are some hearty and heartbreaking scenes from those days.

Crossing the Susquehanna at Perryville, a $1 ride in 1906. (EPFL)

An auto ferry over the Susquehanna. Father made it, in nine hours in 1908. (EPFL)

Members of the Baltimore motorcycle club on a 1911 outing. (EPFL)

Hitting the high road, and the bumps, during the nineteen-oughts. (ML)

Why horses survived. (MDT)

Miss Caroline Evans tinkers with her stalled roadster in 1916. (CPM)

A downtown dies . . . and is reborn

Like a tragic postscript to a calm world, flames rose high over Baltimore city the night of February 7, 1904. Starting in a dry goods company near the center of the city, the holocaust, fanned by high winds, raged virtually out of control for about 30 hours.

When it was over, 1,500 structures had been gutted or simply disappeared. One hundred and forty acres was devastated and about $125 million (in the hard coin of the silver age, or more like a billion or two today) had gone up in smoke.

Amazingly, there was no known loss of life.

The freakish blaze, which probably reached 2,500 degrees, burned around two low-lying banking houses, leaving them relatively undamaged. Safes fell through gutted floors, were allowed to cool for weeks, to save millions in negotiable securities and cash. Recovery was rapid; insurance losses, immense.

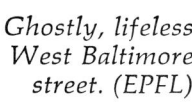

The city revives, with trolley service renewed. (EPFL)

The gutted B&O Railroad headquarters, "pride and joy" of John W. Garrett. (EPFL)

A busy telephone repair crew at rest on Boston street, Canton, the year of the great fire. (CPM)

Fire-streaked skyscrapers looking north from the harbor. (EPFL)

Ghostly, lifeless West Baltimore street. (EPFL)

The golden steamboat days

Bay passenger travel on a regular schedule dates back to at least 1813 but reached its heyday from the Civil War through the 1920's. Literally dozens of independent lines treated passengers to breezy, food-filled trips to points on the Bay, with one of the favorites being a voyage to Old Point Comfort, Va. and the gaslit splendours of the Hygeia hotel. Best known of all the lines was the Baltimore Steam Packet Company, (Old Bay Line). It lasted from 1840 to 1960.

Cottage style lights like this one guarded the shores. This is the Hooper strait lighthouse, removed to St. Michael's in the modern era. (CBMM)

Who could miss a Bay Line trip who saw this? (LC)

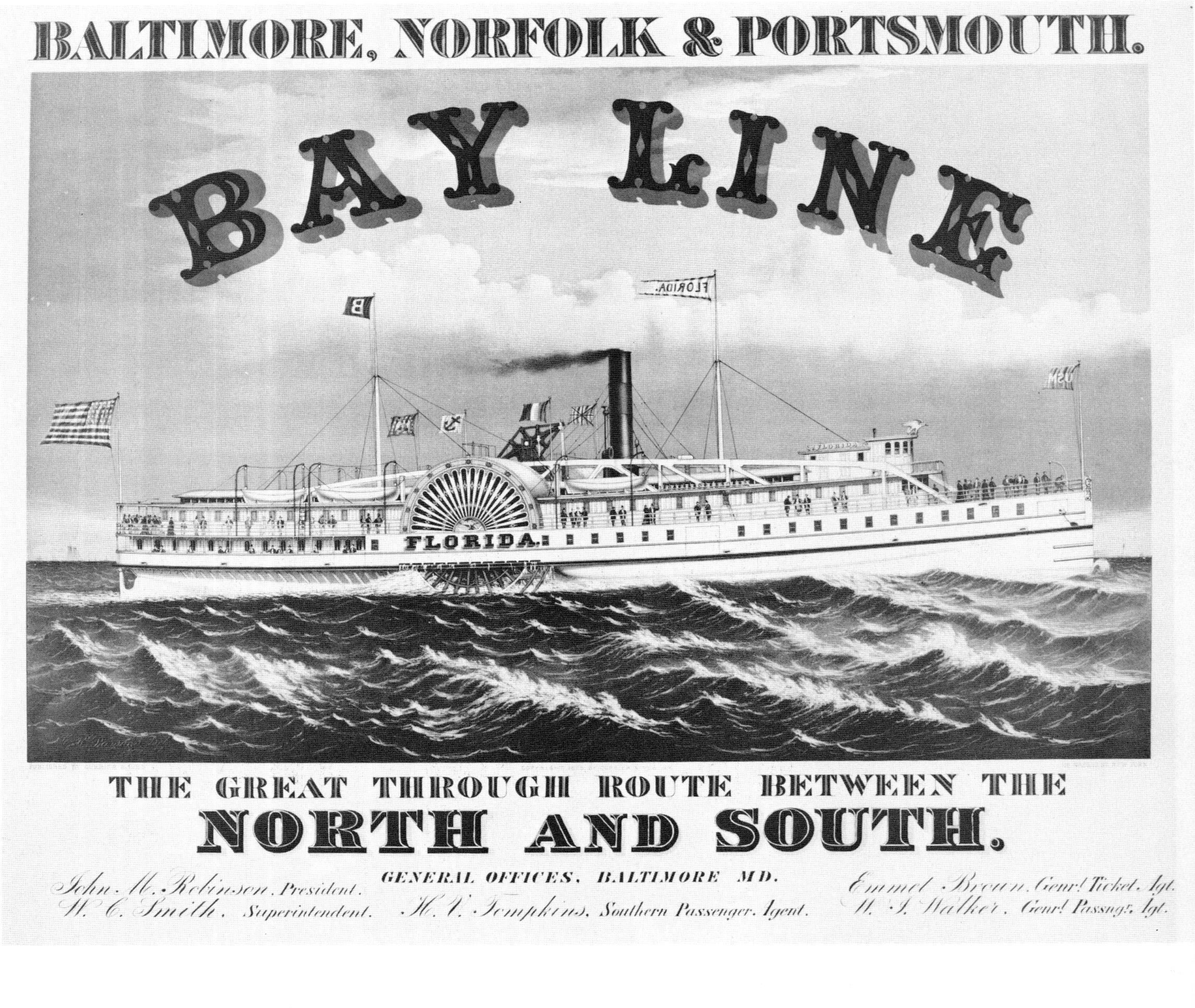

The pretty Louise *collided with another steamer off Seven Foot knoll. Fourteen lives were lost in the 1890 accident. (SHSA)*

One of the last of the greats and one of the largest, the City of Baltimore. *It burned in 1937. (EPFL)*

The fondly-remembered Emma Giles, *sailing serenly for Tolchester. (EPFL)*

Piers of the Potomac and Rappahannock when Light street was widened in the western harbor. (EPFL)

Tremors of the age to come

Early in the century there were some Maryland samples of the world that was to come—a world of film and wars, the space age and civilian disasters. Here are some samples from the Maryland memory book.

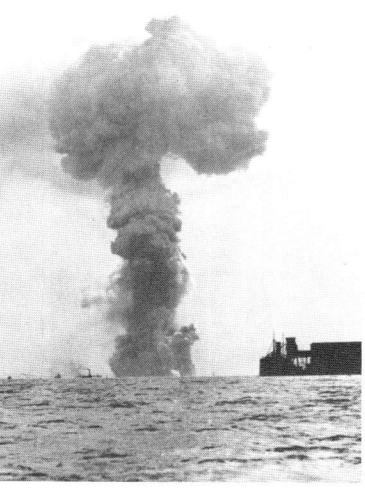

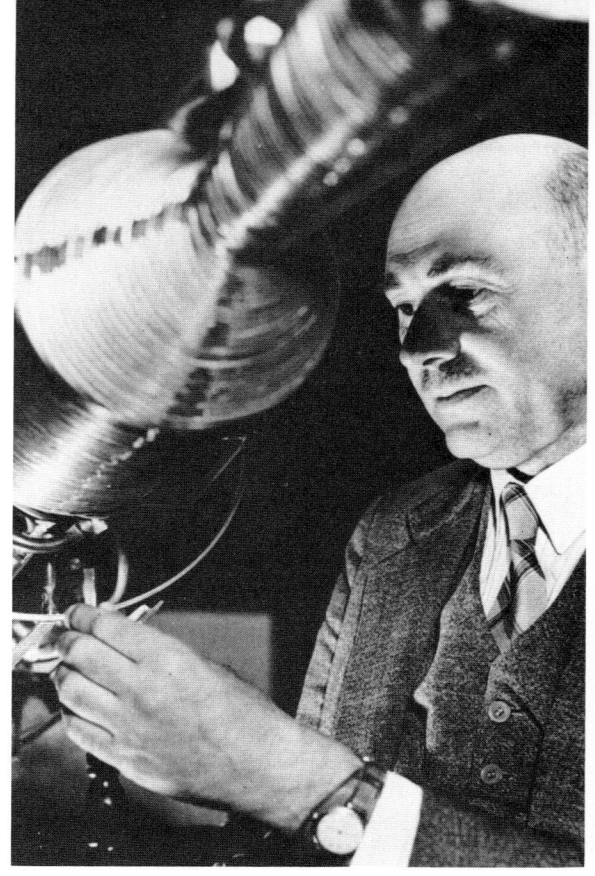

Space pioneer Robert Goddard conducted one of the first formal rocketry tests in history at Aberdeen in November, 1918. (NASA, 1940 photo)

The munitions ship, Alum Chine, *explodes in the lower Patapsco, killing 33 and injuring 60 in March, 1913, a blast heard in Wilmington, Del. (EPFL)*

The Sun *announces the sinking of the* Titanic *in the north Atlantic which took 1,500 lives but not that of Miss Carter, of Baltimore, on board. (BS)*

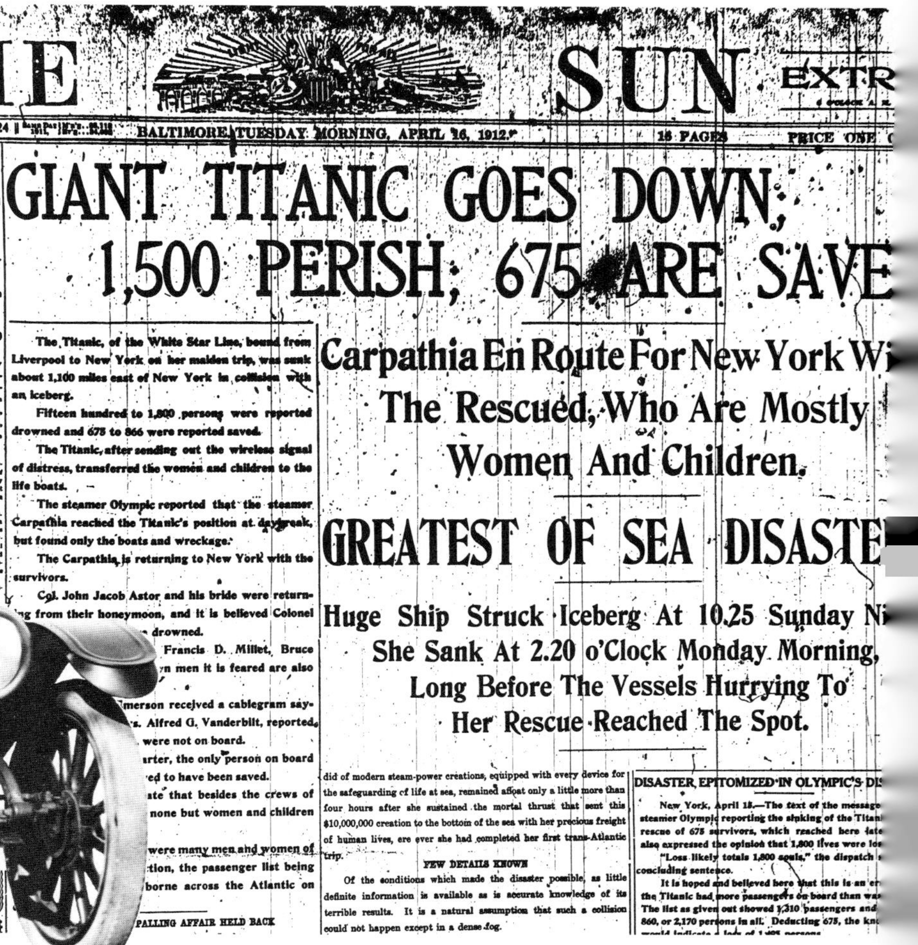

THE SUN EXTR

VOLUME CD—NO. 152. BALTIMORE, TUESDAY MORNING, APRIL 16, 1912. 18 PAGES PRICE ONE C

GROUND RENTS.

OPENED WITH AXES

Clash Between Militia And Police Precedes Cook County Democratic Convention.

TWO MEETINGS IS RESULT

SIDES WERE ENJOINED

GIANT TITANIC GOES DOWN; 1,500 PERISH; 675 ARE SAVE

The Titanic, of the White Star Line, bound from Liverpool to New York on her maiden trip, was sunk about 1,100 miles east of New York in collision with an iceberg.

Fifteen hundred to 1,800 persons were reported drowned and 675 to 866 were reported saved.

The Titanic, after sending out the wireless signal of distress, transferred the women and children to the life boats.

The steamer Olympic reported that the steamer Carpathia reached the Titanic's position at daybreak, but found only the boats and wreckage.

The Carpathia is returning to New York with the survivors.

Col. John Jacob Astor and his bride were returning from their honeymoon, and it is believed Colonel ... drowned.

... Francis D. Millet, Bruce ... men it is feared are also ...

... merson received a cablegram say... Alfred G. Vanderbilt, reported, ... were not on board.

... arter, the only person on board ... ed to have been saved.

... ate that besides the crews of ... none but women and children ...

... were many men and women of ... tion, the passenger list being ... borne across the Atlantic on

... PALLING AFFAIR HELD BACK

Carpathia En Route For New York Wi

The Rescued, Who Are Mostly Women And Children.

GREATEST OF SEA DISASTE

Huge Ship Struck Iceberg At 10.25 Sunday Ni

She Sank At 2.20 o'Clock Monday Morning, Long Before The Vessels Hurrying To Her Rescue Reached The Spot.

did of modern steam-power creations, equipped with every device for the safeguarding of life at sea, remained afloat only a little more than four hours after she sustained the mortal thrust that sent this $10,000,000 creation to the bottom of the sea with her precious freight of human lives, ere ever she had completed her first trans-Atlantic trip.

FEW DETAILS KNOWN

Of the conditions which made the disaster possible, as little definite information is available as is accurate knowledge of its terrible results. It is a natural assumption that such a collision could not happen except in a dense fog.

DISASTER EPITOMIZED IN OLYMPIC'S DIS

New York, April 15.—The text of the message steamer Olympic reporting the sinking of the Titan rescue of 675 survivors, which reached here late also expressed the opinion that 1,800 lives were los

"Loss likely totals 1,800 souls," the dispatch concluding sentence.

It is hoped and believed here that this is an er the Titanic had more passengers on board than was The list as given out showed 1,310 passengers and 860, or 2,170 persons in all. Deducting 675, the kn ...

BLACK PATTI

PURNELL ART CO., 224 N. HOWARD ST.

AUDITORIUM

Chasing the dastards in a 1915 touring car. (EPFL)

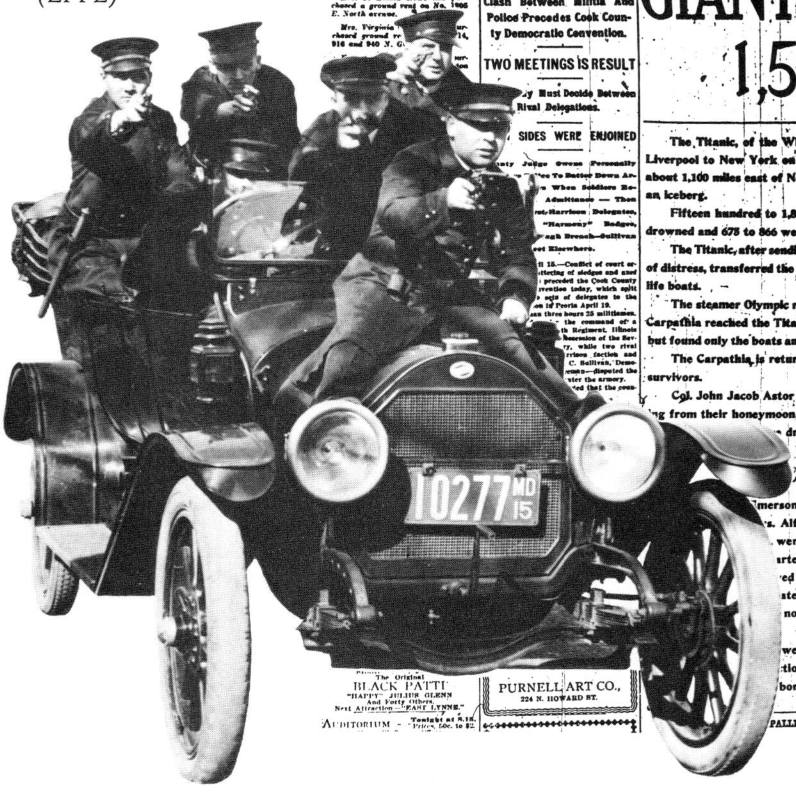

An era ends

The curtain came down on European society in August, 1914 and Maryland was soon to prepare for its first world conflict.

Robert D. Carter, last police marshal of Baltimore, looks ready for trouble in a World War I era parade. (EPFL)

Insignia of the 110th Field Artillery, a segment of Maryland's 29th ("Blue and Gray") Division in World War I. Division lost more than 1,000 killed, 4,500 injured in Meuse-Argonne campaign. (BS)

A mess kit clean up at Fort Meade training center. (LC)

Maryland's 115th field division embarks for Gay Paree from Camp Steuart, Va. (BS)

Joy sweeps a downtown Baltimore mob as "it's over, over there!" (BS)

1918 — 1941
PROGRESS AND POVERTY

FOR MANY AMERICANS, and indeed, for the world, the 1920's and 1930's have been the most influential decades of the Twentieth Century.

Revolutions in literature, the graphic arts, broadcast media and the social sciences occurred. So did the giant specter of the Depression and the rise of dictatorships under Adolf Hitler, certainly the most important historic examples that affect American politics and foreign policy respectively.

For nearly three quarters of the period, Maryland was under the leadership of handsome, able Albert C. Ritchie, an attorney who in a decade moved from Baltimore city's legal department into a 15-year term in the governor's mansion.

Much of this era was dominated by an epochal fight against Prohibition and the Eighteenth Amendment, with Ritchie and Maryland as a whole taking stances as one of the nation's loudest "wets." Before Ritchie left office in 1935, the State's distillers and brewers were back into the beer and liquor business, with high hopes that it would turn the Depression around and halt the breadlines by crowding the saloons.

Recovery was very slow, although there is some feeling that Baltimore weathered the storm better than most other major manufacturing centers, according to some economic historians.

Maryland farm production declined during the era as rural populations took to the cities in the face of the agricultural slump of the early 1920's and the disastrous collapse of commodities in the early 1930's.

Some things flourished, however: higher education, which began to provide itself with adequate physical plants that could service the new age of specialization and technology in road building. By the late Thirties, some experts rated Maryland's road system as one of the nation's best.

Franklin Roosevelt's "New Deal" found fertile ground in the state—with the building of Greenbelt, Prince Georges county model planned town for the low income family and in widespread use of federal programs creating a rash of WPA post offices, historical murals, and public works associated with housing, forestry, recreation and travel.

During one week in 1929, Baltimore had 20 flagpole sitters, rage of the year. Avon Foreman, who was the first, received a letter of appreciation from Mayor Broening. (BS)

A political highlight of the period was the attempt by New Dealers to "purge" senior senator Millard Tydings. It failed and as a political cause celebre it probably ranks second only to the "court packing" scheme of Franklin Roosevelt.

At the end of the era, Maryland industry was set for a war-born boom to come in the next decade. Many graceful old ways, killed off by the Depression, vanished from locales, probably forever.

Millard Tydings proved unpurgable. (ML)

"We want beer!" shouted the college boys from a hillside as Herbert Hoover hit the campaign trail in October, 1932 at Baltimore's Mount Royal station. A week later he was snowed under by the ebullient FDR. (AAB)

Builders and Buildings

Maryland's construction pace quickened across the state as the Twenties roared in and was kept alive through federal aids during the Thirties slump.

Dedicating Mayor Preston's masterpiece. (EPFL)

Vast physical expansion of the University of Maryland at College Park began in the mid-1930's. Long-time university president Dr. H. C. "Curly" Byrd masterminded the show, is flanked here by federal public works officials. (EPFL)

John Russell Pope's classic Baltimore Museum of Art building, built for $1 million on land donated by Johns Hopkins University in 1928. (AAB)

Mayor James Preston earned a national name as a "take over" type executive when he cleaned out Baltimore's hoary court district, constructing one of the first urban renewal projects designed to cope with automobiles. (EPFL)

The Maryland National Bank building going up in Baltimore while the stock market went down in 1929. (EPFL)

The great achievers

These Marylanders and Maryland residents won world acclaim during the Twentieth Century for outstanding achievements in the arts and sciences, religion, sports and medicine.

James, Cardinal Gibbons (1834–1921), marched behind the casket of Abraham Lincoln in 1865, went on to become the confidant of Presidents and the most beloved Catholic prelate in American history. (MR)

Henrietta Szold (1860–1945), a bright star of west Baltimore's intellectual community, founded the Hadassah movement, pioneered in international health and spent her last years rescuing hundreds of central and eastern European Jews from Hitler's SS troops. (BS)

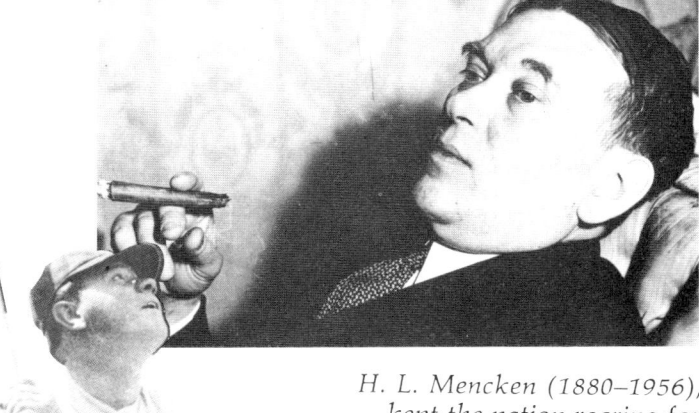

H. L. Mencken (1880–1956), kept the nation roaring for more than 40 years as he pummeled politicians and provincialism in the arts. He did nothing to dilute his curmudgeonly and crusty legend by writing his own epitaph. It asks that those left behind "forgive some sinner and wink your eye at some homely girl." (EPFL)

Rosa Ponselle, Metropolitan Opera diva, made her debut with Enrico Caruso in 1919, became the greatest Aida of her generation and retired to train proteges and enrich Maryland music as artistic director of the Baltimore Opera Company. (BOC)

George Herman (Babe) Ruth (1895–1948), the Beethoven of the bat, hit 714 home runs in the major leagues, rising from humble beginnings to become the greatest New York Yankee of them all. (LBM)

Luxury notes for the bon ton

Maryland traditions were kept alive during the financial stringency and the railroads, as yet unthreatened by anything but a token air passenger service, rose to their final glory.

Cloche hats on the heads and Deer Park mineral water from the B&O's own spring on the tables were the feature aboard the Martha Washington, the first successfully air-conditioned dining car. (BORRM)

A B&O dining car crew and their steward in immaculate whites. (BORRM)

An early 1930's roadster, complete with rumble seat, calls on Amoco. The price was 17 cents—two cents off for cash. (AAB)

A mass of sports-minded humanity gathers on the slopes of the J. W. Y. Martin estate for an early 1930's running of the Maryland Hunt Cup, timber classic founded in 1894. (AAB)

"Billy Barton" legendary timber racer thunders home before the 1926 hunt cup race. (AAB)

Riding to the hounds over Maryland farmland, a tradition dating back to the late Seventeenth Century. (AAB)

A 1933 pony show at the state fairgrounds, Timonium. (EPFL)

Traffic . . . parking . . . and problems

Henry Ford had a better idea in the 1920's but the arrival of locomotion for the millions was not without headaches. Some of the blessings of internal combustion.

The Western Shore Transit Company operated this shining specimen for a bus ride from Solomons Island to Annapolis in the mid thirties. (EPFL)

Parking on both sides and traffic both ways, the standard solution through the Thirties at Cambridge along Race street and elsewhere. (EPFL)

All-day parking for 25 cents in the late thirties off Guilford avenue. (EPFL)

The new art form—auto dumps—circa 1936. (EPFL)

Headquarters for Maryland auto sales from 1920 to 1950—Baltimore's Mount Royal avenue. (EPFL)

The auto age arrives in Taneytown, Carroll county, along with paving on October 2, 1920. (EPFL)

Roll out the barrel and put it on bricks—a 1921 traffic aid. (EPFL)

Woe to the speedster who met state trooper James R. Miller in goggles and natty atire in the Thirties. (AAB)

Traveling in packs and showing off

Locomotion soon to disappear from the scenery but everyday affairs through the 1920's.

The shiny new status symbol was not to be denied and somehow it was more fun when everyone did it at once.

Southern Maryland tobacco hogsheads moved to market by bullock cart. (EPFL)

The Western Maryland's Baltimore train in a Hagerstown call. (LC)

Flag-decked rovers of the Yellow Cab Company advertise the lowest fares in town on a shady Roland Park lane, Baltimore. (ML)

Your phone book came by horse cart in 1919. (CPM)

Easter Sunday turnout in 1931 along Baltimore's Charles street. (AAB)

Chloroform and alcohol for baby, a lingering patent medicine note in Hagerstown. (LC)

An autocade arrives at College Park for a "Farmer's Day" celebration in the mid-1920's. (ML)

Bounties of the land and sea

Eastern shore acres and the state's 3,200 miles of coastline continued to enrich American dinner tables. Sometimes there were some surprises.

Simple pleasures between the wars: A spring stroll through Baltimore's Sherwood Gardens a few months before Pearl Harbor. (AAB)

Famed Eastern Shore tomatoes arrive by the boatload at a Baltimore pier. (AAB)

A state staple for more than 300 years, tobacco is auctioned in a warehouse. (AAB)

The ultimate in old swimming holes, Muddy Creek falls in Swallow Falls state forest. (EPFL)

A 500-pound shark, 10 feet long captured in the Patuxent. (EPFL)

Oyster tongers at Rock Point on the Bay, 1941. (LC)

A clam shucker prepares a catch for packing. (AAB)

A wall of water... March, 1936

Western Maryland's spring freshets turned into a torrent of destruction during a 48-hour period in March, 1936, as the swollen Potomac burst its banks and raged through low-lying towns. Some scenes from the disaster, which left thousands homeless.

Carnage in the Cumberland central business district. (EPFL)

Water rescues in Hancock were frequent. (EPFL)

The flood at Green Spring, Washington county. (EPFL)

Billions of tons of water cut through Ocean City's barrier beach to Sinepuxent bay during the hurricane of 1933, but the freak of nature proved a benefit to sports fishing. (BS)

Two bridges at Harpers Ferry, one gone, the other weighted with freight cars in hopes of saving it. (EPFL)

Things to do in the threadbare thirties

When $30 billion in stock equities went up in smoke in the great price slide of 1929–1931, it spelled out new lifestyles. About 15 Maryland banks went to the wall and soon people without money outnumbered those with it. Relief families were living on 3.5 cents a meal, but you could still have fun and learn a few things as some of these pictures prove.

Keeping cool in the 1930's mean going to the movies and this Richard Barthlemess thriller. (EPFL)

A rainy day and a wet welcome at Pimlico for the Hagenbeck-Wallace circus in 1934. (AAB)

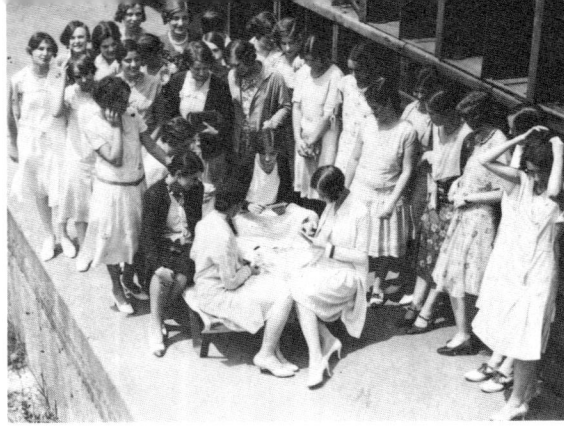

Card packs were 10 cents and the bridge craze at its height during this lunch break at the Point Breeze plant of Western Electric. (EPFL)

Local color: visitors relaxing at a Frederick furniture auction. (LC)

The Junior League follies—1936 edition—a tap dancing octet in the Belvedere hotel ballroom. (AAB)

Reading the menu. The suitcase was cardboard and the prices eye-popping with a ham sandwich exactly 5 cents. (AAB)

Middies head for Memorial Stadium's goal posts after a triumph over Notre Dame in November, 1936. (SO)

Jack Dunn, who won seven championships in International league ball, was czar of Baltimore baseball from 1907 until 1928. (BS)

Seabiscuit thunders home a half a length ahead of War Admiral, a Pimlico classic match race in the late 1930's. (BNA)

Sudlersville native Jimmy Foxx, indestructible major league catcher, and first baseman looked like this from the pitcher's mound. (BNA)

Handcraft classes sponsored by the National Youth Administration helped students learn to make nets for needy fishermen. (EPFL)

Mrs. Eugenia Smith gets instruction in bean canning from a Farmers Home Administration field supervisor. (LC)

Civilian Conservation Corps boys got a healthy tan fixing up the nation's first monument to George Washington, built in 1827 by western Marylanders near Boonsboro. (AAB)

Smokers kept parts of Southern Maryland at work. A St. Marys grower with product. (EPFL)

Waiting out the depression

The business collapse of the 1930's, severest for the nation in probably 50 years, caused widespread hardship. Tens of thousands of citizens went without work for years on end. The great slump was particularly hard on rural areas and on Western Maryland whose extractive industries depended to a heavy degree on industrial finance.

Striking Cambridge canners put up a telephone pole sign saying they can't live on $9.80 a week. (LC)

Jobs were a memory for these Garrett county farm folk in November, 1936. (LC)

Government-sponsored work helped many. Four 11-ton light vessels are crafted by Curtis Bay artisans in 1937. (EPFL)

Docked oyster tongers and dredges symbolize the oyster famine of 1935–1936 when severe weather halted harvest. (EPFL)

An abandoned general store and hotel in western Maryland. (LC)

Waiting for a job—any job—at a Route 1 truckstop in 1940. (LC)

Festivals and fun notes

Anniversaries have always been important to tradition-oriented Marylanders and two of their biggest bashes between the wars were Maryland's 300th anniversary and the 100th year that the B&O came around the bend. A costumed pageant in Memorial Stadium was a highlight of the 1634–1934 doings. An "Iron Horse Fair" at Halethorpe, Baltimore county, signalled the railroad centennial before 46,000 spectators in 1927.

This reproduction of *The Ark*, the ship that founded Maryland colony, was a feature of the 300th. (AAB)

Colonial-garbed beauties deliver the first Tercentenary pageant ticket to Baltimore's Mayor Howard Jackson. (EPFL)

Engineers and firemen don period attire for the railroad fair. (ML)

The DeWitt Clinton, last word in 1830's locomotion, thrills Iron Horse Fair crowd. (AAB)

A balmy Ocean City day in the late 1930's when today's $300 Panama went for about $10. (EPFL)

The last years of peace

By 1936 and 1937, European storm clouds were distinctly audible in the eastern United States. These pictures illustrate something of what was to come.

A Pan American clipper ship is readied for service to Bermuda in 1937, heralding rise of passenger aviation. (AAB)

The German cruiser Emden *put on a Baltimore harbor show, evidence of growing Nazi power at sea in 1936. (AAB)*

West Pointers inspect one of the big ones at Aberdeen Proving Ground, Harford county. Soon they would get to use them. (EPFL)

June Week hi-jinks at Annapolis the same year with Miss Janet Cuneen presenting the colors to Midshipman Harry B. Hahn as Rear Admiral D. Foote Sellers looks on. (EPFL)

Maryland wets rejoiced at this scene. Beer was back in keg and bottle by the mid-thirties. The keg house of the vanished Bismarck brand. (AAB)

1941 — 1976
WAR AND PEACE

THE MARYLAND STORY in World War II and after is one of thunderous, precipitate expansion.

What had been a prosperous ring of largely agricultural counties with a few major marketing centers and a single great manufacturing city became a wholly modern texture, complex, far larger and difficult to manage.

The war gave the impetus. Millions of people poured into the middle-Atlantic shelf, nerve center of the war effort and all but overwhelmed housing and transient services.

More or less the same thing happened in every state, of course, but Maryland had some advantage over many of the others in that it had four major U. S. Army centers, a national service academy, the world's largest tidewater steel mill and perhaps most important of all, a mechanical tradition of "coping." When the war was over, many of the state's new transplanted citizens from the central Alleghanies and the South stayed on. The added manpower, largely unskilled, was not regarded as a major resource by political forces. It was also accompanied by freakish population changes that swept through the central state, leaving the Eastern Shore and Western Maryland largely untouched.

Montgomery county, an almost wholly agricultural doze of farmland and about 30,000 souls as recently as 1930, in a little under three decades became a 600,000-person complex of high-income wealth larger than Kansas City, Mo. Sprawling Prince Georges county grew even faster. In western Baltimore county the new Social Security center, perhaps the largest government agency in the world on one site, acted as an employment magnet, pulling once remote suburban villages like Catonsville, Randallstown, Ellicott City and Woodlawn into the metropolitan orbit. By about 1952, the old Maryland balance between agriculture and manufacturing had been shattered, after dominating the economy for something like 125 years.

In the early 1950's, service industries began to outrank manufacturing as a creator of jobs and as a money machine. The new accent in Maryland was not on people who made things or grew things to sell, it was on people who did things for other people, usually other businesses.

So it has remained since the first large wave of happy GI's ran out of the gates at Fort Meade, Camp Ritchie, Bainbridge, Aberdeen-Edgewood and Holabird a victorious generation ago.

The flag flies over the Fort McHenry National Monument as it has for 179 years, guarding the only major American port that has never flown a foreign flag. (WHO)

Maryland in World War II

Blackouts and gas rationing, draft cards and jobs were ahead for Marylanders as the 1940's opened and France folded under a lightning German "blitzkreig."

State industries won about $1 billion in new contracts as the defense effort escalated. Large scale hiring, about 100,000 jobs within a few months time, blossomed for the first time on any large scale since the 1920's. This put a severe strain on housing and the transportation systems. Emergency housing mushroomed. The Baltimore-Washington corridor and its Philadelphia diagonal through Aberdeen had every known rank and uniform of the Allied powers.

A "WAC" keeps the camera equipment straight at the Fort Holabird east Baltimore signal depot. (EPFL)

Raking the lawn, a wartime housing scene from Middle River, 1942. (LC)

Chauffeurs wait patiently by their sleek limousines in 1943 as the brass launches another warship on the Patapsco. (LC)

Whistles screamed and fireboats sprayed water as Mrs. Henry Wallace launched the S. S. Patrick Henry, the first of 2,700 "Liberty" ships. It was crafted at the Bethlehem-Fairfield shipyards. (BS)

A 1944 spectacular, Old Oriole park in northeast Baltimore burns down to the last bleacher. (BS)

An assault training exercise on the beach at Betterton, 1942. (WHO)

The Duke of Kent shown addressing about 18,000 defense workers at the Martin plant, Middle River, in August 1941. (WHO)

Baltimore harbor, jammed stem to stern with ships during the 1946 dock strike. (WHO)

The home front gives an exhuberant welcome to V-J day in downtown Baltimore. (BS)

President Roosevelt and Governor O'Conor plug up for a big gun salute during a visit to the Aberdeen armaments center. (WHO)

Champions in longevity

Maryland has seen 10 presidents of the United States since 1920 but only 8 governors, which should say something about political longevity in Annapolis. About every other governor has evolved into a sort of fixed symbol of a decade. The four champs shown here served the state for a total of 47 years.

Albert C. Ritchie (1876–1936), was one of the few men who ever said "no" to FDR, declining to run as vice presidential candidate in the 1932 shoo-in. His four popular terms started in 1920. (EPFL)

J. Millard Tawes, Somerset countian and Eastern Shoreman of the deepest dye, was state executive from 1959 through 1967, boosted state aid to the counties and accomplishing the first public accommodation law in the South. (ML)

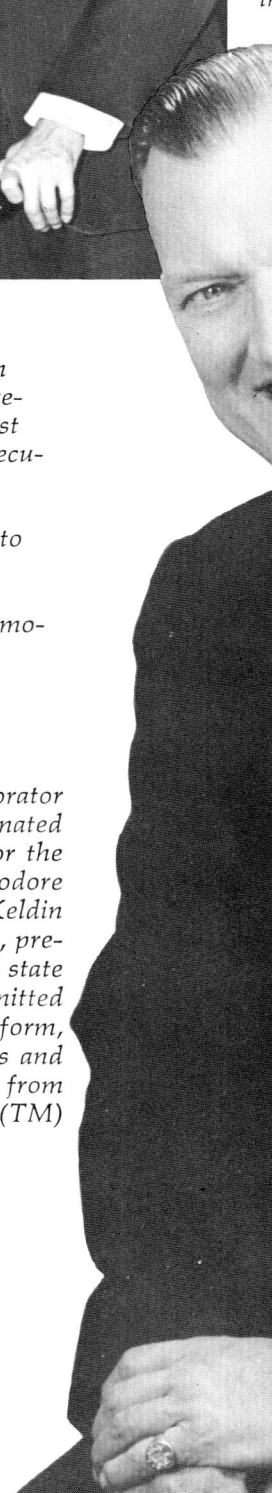

A popular orator who nominated Eisenhower for the presidency, Theodore R. McKeldin (1900–1975), presided over a state program committed to budget reform, public works and road-building, from 1951 to 1959. (TM)

Herbert R. O'Conor (1896–1960), Governor from 1939 to 1947, was a master of Maryland's Democratic machinery and led the state during World War II, finishing 52 years of public service in the United States Senate. (EPFL)

Modern culture in new settings

The state's artistic resources were broadened in the modern period by a combination of private philanthrophy, community spirit and help from the government sector. Older institutions enlarged their programs and their appeal and new ones were founded, surprisingly, in the face of rapid cost escalations for all sorts of entertainment, performance and training in the arts.

Focal point for Charles Center and headquarters for Broadway productions and the legitimate stage, the Mechanic Theater. (AAB)

The Baltimore symphony, in choral concert at the Lyric Theater. Founded in 1916 as one of the world's first municipally supported symphonic groups, the orchestra in modern times inaugurated a summer season at the spectacular Merriweather Post pavilion, Columbia. (BS)

The Washington County Museum of Fine Arts at Hagerstown, Center of Western Maryland culture since the 1930's. (AAB)

The Harford Opera theater, feature of summertime at Goucher College and Bel Air, in performance with "The Barber of Seville." (HOT)

Burned out in a disastrous 1974 fire, Baltimore's regional theater, Center Stage, was reborn within a year in a restored college auditorium. First nighters greet Moliere's "Tartuffe." (CS)

Great moments from the sports pages

Major league franchises in both baseball and football came back to Maryland in the postwar period and Baltimore-based teams made history, while Pimlico's racing luster went undimmed into its second century.

Secretariat, 1975 triple crown winner, heading for the Preakness winner's circle at Pimlico. (BNA)

World turf talent thunders home in the Laurel International, a major racing feature and celebrity haunt, founded in 1952. (AAB)

A world first: a reigning queen of England watches an American football game. At left is Dr. Wilson Elkins, University of Maryland president; at right, Governor McKeldin. The Terrapins downed the NC Tarheels 21 to 7 in October, 1957. (ML)

The Baltimore Colts capture the National Football League title in the famous 1958 "sudden death" overtime, 23 to 17 over the New York Giants. Alan Ameche scores the touchdown. The great Johnnie Unitas, No. 19, has just set up the play. (WWP)

Tidings of great joy in April, 1954 as the Orioles return of the American League after 52 years of minor league play. Richard Nixon tossed the first ball and Orioles won 3 to 1 over the Chicago White Sox. (BS)

Earl Weaver, Oriole manager, gets a dunking at final 1970 World Series game, a 4 to 1 triumph over Cincinnati. The Birds made it four years earlier in 1966, too. (BNA)

Lacrosse action on the Homewood field at Johns Hopkins University in 1966. Hopkins stickmen have won nearly 30 championships since the 1920's. (BS)

Signposts of the mind

These men helped to continue the tradition of eminence for Maryland science, education and the law.

Dr. John M. T. Finney (1863–1942), was dean by acclamation of Maryland's medical professionals and surgeon to the mighty and the humble, including Mrs. Evalyn Walsh McLean, of "Hope Diamond" fame. (EPFL)

Arthur O. Lovejoy (1873–1962), of the Johns Hopkins University became a legend to generations of philosophy students, won world fame with publication of "The Great Chain of Being." (ML)

Justice Thurgood Marshall, of Baltimore, argued the famous Brown vs the Board of Education *case that ended "separate but equal" educational treatment, became the first black solicitor general of the United States and the first black member of the supreme tribunal. (BS)*

Making it work during the boom years

By the 1950's, the state was ready to perform in the area of major public works and private renewal. Collectively, these projects cost billions, affected millions by linking trade centers, providing new housing for people, business and industry, new power sources and ways to reach and study the Chesapeake Bay.

Millions of East Coast drivers welcomed this facility in the 1950's—the Baltimore harbor tunnel, replacing the most notorious bottleneck in the middle Atlantic. (MDT)

Flanked by Mayor Thomas D'Alesandro, Jr., left and Hunter Moss, developer, right, J. Jefferson Miller (seated) director of the multi-million dollar Charles Center redevelopment, sign a contract for the Baltimore master plan in April, 1957. (CCI)

Baltimore harbor looked like this on the nation's 200th anniversary. The Frigate **Constellation** is moored at center right. The 40-story headquarters tower of the United States Fidelity and Guaranty Company dominates horizon at left, while World Trade Center rises at right. (CCI)

President Truman arrives to launch Baltimore-Washington International airport in a 1950 ceremony and is met by Mayor D'Alesandro. (BS)

One week before Dallas: John F. Kennedy at Elkton, opening Interstate 95 into Delaware, now the JFK Expressway. At right, Governor Millard Tawes. (ML)

Maryland's first atomic power plant, the Calvert Cliffs facility of the Baltimore Gas & Electric Company. It generated 5.7 billion kilowatt hours the first year. (BGE)

Mayor J. Harold Grady is at the throttle, bulldozing a ground-breaking for Charles Center in August, 1961. (CCI)

Twin views of the 4.1-mile Bay behomoth, the William Preston Lane memorial bridge, first, below in its 1952 single span version and left, with second span added early in the 1970's. (MDT)

James Rouse, mortgage banker and developer, second from right, launches a model for the City of Columbia, Howard county. In less than a decade, the 12,000-acre project had 40,000 residents, 700 businesses and industries. (RC)

Downtown Columbia by night. (RC)

Dreamed of as long ago as the Seventeenth Century, the C&D canal shortened the Philadelphia-Baltimore shipping route by 280 miles. (AAB)

Dundalk Marine Terminal, number one weapon of the Maryland Port Administration, in boosting world trade in and out of Baltimore harbor. (MPA)

Giants of business and industry

If they managed to struggle into and out of the great depression of the 1930's, many Maryland businesses often grew into international operations and frequently offered new approaches to marketing, manufacturing or finance that developed nation-wide. Here are some of the leaders in the effort since the earliest days of the Twentieth Century.

Alexander E. Duncan (1878–1972), founded Commercial Credit Company in 1912 with $300,000 and a new approach to the problems of merchant finance. When he retired as head of the financing giant in 1958 it had total resources of $1.7 billion. (CCC)

Miracles of management were performed by C. P. McCormick (1896–1970), who took over a faltering depression business and increased its volume 20 times. McCormick & Co., Inc., is now the world's largest spice processor. (MC)

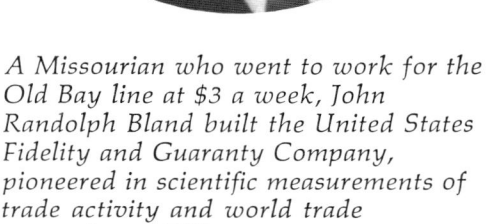

A Missourian who went to work for the Old Bay line at $3 a week, John Randolph Bland built the United States Fidelity and Guaranty Company, pioneered in scientific measurements of trade activity and world trade promotion. (USF)

Glenn L. Martin (1886–1955), started a career in aviation only six years after the first flight at Kitty Hawk, N.C. and created the giant Martin Company of World War II aviation fame. (EPFL)

A native of Brooklyn, N. Y., Thomas W. Pangborn (1880–1967), founded one of the world's largest blast cleaning and dust control firms in 1912. An educational philanthrophist, he was America's highest ranking Catholic layman. (BS)

Raymond J. Funkhouser (1889–1968), was a conglomerate businessman before it was fashionable, at one time owned and controlled 18 corporations, including Ruberoid. The colorful Hagerstown publisher was a leader for prohibition in Western Maryland. (BS)

Howard Bruce (1880–1961), organized the Baltimore National Bank in the depths of the depression, August, 1933, and brought it into regional leadership, through mergers as Fidelity-Baltimore National and Maryland National Bank, since 1961, the state's largest. (MNB)

Regarded as one of the most brilliant investment analysts in America, Glyndon-native T. Rowe Price built the $6 billion investment funds that bear his name. His business career started in 1919. (TP)

Robert D. Black

Alonzo G. Decker, Jr.

These two men built Maryland's largest manufacturing firm, The Black & Decker Manufacturing Company. Black joined the company in 1917 and Decker in 1922. Both headed the Towson-based tool empire in successive chairmanships from 1956 until 1975. Sales sextupled to nearly $650 million. (BD)

Jacob Blaustein (1892–1970), pioneered the "visible" auto station pump and also the drive-through station, creating vast American Oil Company and serving as a Standard of Indiana director. (BI)

Some serene spots

Though state population grew 26 per cent in the 1960's, peace and tradition could still be found along Maryland byways and sometimes in the heart of cities.

Deep Creek lake, a boating haven at midsummer. (WHO)

An Amish shop at New Market, an unchanged idiom of a picturesque people. (AAB)

Property restoration became the byword in Annapolis, Easton, Frederick, Port Tobacco, Chestertown, Westminster and other centers after the war. One of the earliest and most charming of the nostalgia trips: Baltimore's Tyson street. (AAB)

A top family attraction on the Eastern Shore, the Chesapeake Bay Maritime Museum at St. Michael's. That's the historic Dodson house on the right. (CBMM)

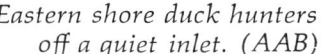

Eastern shore duck hunters off a quiet inlet. (AAB)

A tranquil ferry trip, traditional mode for getting there in southern and eastern Maryland. (AAB)

. . . and the Bay's legendary larder

Oysters, clams and crabs and the glamorous boats that catch them were surviving themes for gourmets, artists and careers for hardworking Maryland watermen in the post-war era.

Oysters on the half shell, with shuckers at work and plenty of customers. (AAB)

The Clarence Lewis, *a typical bay bugeye boat makes a "lick," dredging over an oyster bed. (AAB)*

Richard Q. (Moco) Yardley, Baltimore Sunpapers *cartoonist, highlighted a short vacation with this playful excuse, part of a series that continued to apply the light touch to Maryland tradition for decades and always kept an eye peeled for crabs or crab cakes. (BS)*

Cold beer and peppery hard crabs, steamed in deep pots, are the number one Bay banquet for many seafood lovers. (AAB)

An oyster catch arrives aboard a skipjack in the mouth of the Choptank and in a driving rain. (AAB)

A graceful skipjack, the Sea Gull skims across the Bay, symbol of vanishing sail power. (AAB)

The Edna Lockwood, built in 1889, a 9-log bugeye rigged canoe, dries its sails at St. Michael's. (CBMM)

A sensation of the somnolent 1950's, the collapse of a wooden grandstand, at Baltimore's Fifth Regiment armory moments before a Sonja Heinie ice show was to have started. More than 250 were injured. (BS)

Triumph and tragedy in the post-war age

The stresses and strains of post-war America did not leave Maryland alone. The youth revolt, racial tensions and political scandals, in fact, seemed to make the state a special victim, polarizing issues and causes in ways that probably brought the state's political reputation lower than it had been in 125 years.

Emerging into the relative peace of the mid-1970's, the state's citizens could be thankful that many of these scenes were over and done with.

Madalyn Murray O'Hare, foe of compulsory prayer in the public schools, doctors a sign in favor of Bible reading. The faithful writhed, but the Supreme Court upheld her case, 8 to 1. (BNA)

Students opposing the Viet Nam war parade in protest. (BS)

Baltimore is shown burning by night in the wake of riots touched off by the murder of Dr. Martin Luther King. (BS)

A tumultuous welcome for Richard Nixon at the peak of his power, a 1970 greeting en route to meet steelworkers in Dundalk. (BS)

The vice presidency of Spiro T. Agnew, former Maryland governor, comes to an end after he entered a nolo contendere plea to a tax evasion charge. (BS)

Black activists are bussed in for demonstrations at Princess Anne in 1964, the start of a four-year Eastern Shore struggle. (BS)

Whitaker Chambers, journalist turned Carroll county farmer, holds a paper announcing climax of the "Pumpkin Papers" case. It led to the imprisonment of Maryland diplomat, Alger Hiss. (BNA)

Young people and the future

Thirty years separate these two College Park scenes and illustrate that student lifestyles are often revealing of their era. Below, in 1941, three Johns Hopkins undergraduates do penance for stealing Testudo, College Park monument to the Terrapin in one of a series of raids on the 400-pound mascot. (ML) At the right, symbolic of the end of the turbulent college generation of the 1960's, two students guard a College Park flag, refusing to allow demonstrators to lower it. The protectors are David Simpson, center and Charles Blocker, right. (WS)

A planning session at Johns Hopkins University's board room in its Centennial year, 1976. Behind the academic council members is a painting of the original 1876 board of trustees for the Hopkins Hospital. At the far right, with council members, is Dr. Steven Muller, University president.

By the mid-1970's, the University of Maryland's downtown Baltimore campus had more than doubled in size through a $50 million building program for the hospital and professional schools. Below, some of the work in progress as it stood in 1974. (BS)

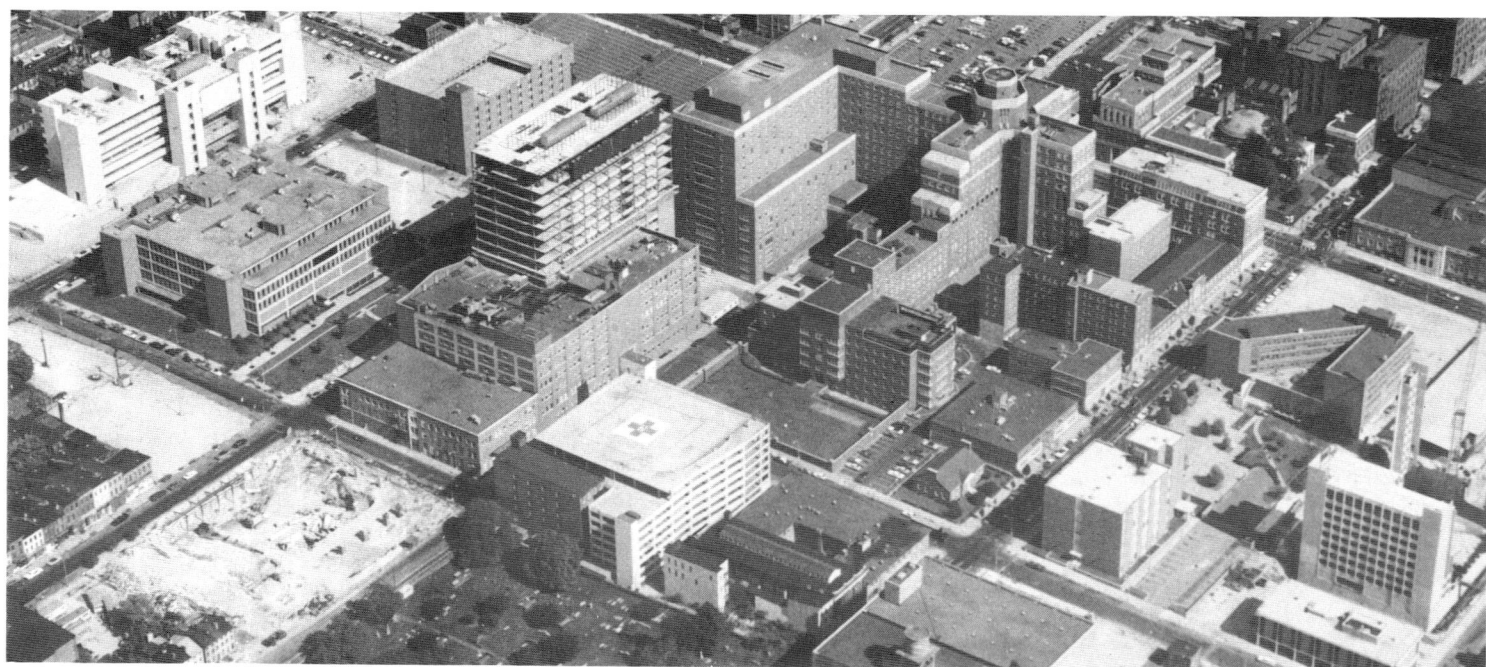

Past and present

A witness to Maryland history and more, Talbot county's Wye Oak, a 400-year-old sentinel that was growing before William Shakespeare had written a single play. (AAB)

Part of a flotilla of nearly three dozen square-rigged ships that arrived in tribute to Maryland and the nation for the 1976 Bicentennial. (MT)

© Morton Tadder

Onward...to the third U.S. century

In line with the growing trend toward outdoor recreation and simple pleasures, state roads authorities began opening the Chesapeake Bay bridge once a year for a "bridge walk" linking both shores. Here are some of the thousands, marching towards the Eastern Shore and the future . . . and perhaps, a remembered past. (BS)

Lady middies at Annapolis, a precedent shattering note for the Bicentennial, repeated at West Point. (NA)

Developers created this panorama of highrises along north Ocean City's gold coast strip: 3,000 condominium units that cost about $200 million. (MW)

ACKNOWLEDGEMENTS

THIS BOOK would not have been possible without the help extended over a period of more than a year by the Enoch Pratt Free Library, whose collections were the source of about one third of the visual material. We are particularly grateful to Ernest Siegel, the library's director, and the staff of the Maryland Room, who gave day-to-day counseling of expert type, including Dr. Morgan Pritchett, head of the department and Mrs. Marjorie Jones and Miss Catherine Kennedy, administrative assistants.

Crucial help in research phases and major material was also provided by the Maryland Historical Society, the Peale Museum, McKeldin Memorial Library of the University of Maryland and the graphics department of the Library of Congress. Our thanks, respectively, to Mrs. Lois McCauley, curator of prints and Mrs. Lynn Cox, graphics assistant, at the society; to Wilbur H. Hunter, director and Paul Amelia, archivist of the museum; to Miss Mary Boccaccio, director of the Maryland room at McKeldin Library and Miss Lauri Sebo, library assistant there, and to Mrs. Renata Shaw, Leroy Bellamy and Jerry Kearns, all of the Library of Congress staff.

Directors and staffs of numerous corporate, public and private collections of Maryland graphics were generous contributors of both photography, prints and in many cases research data. These included Mrs. Theodore Roosevelt McKeldin and Mrs. A. Aubrey Bodine, Mrs. Vera Leclercq and Willis Cook, both of the Baltimore & Ohio Railroad Museum; James Wilson of the Steamship Historical Society of America; Mary Ann Kennedy, of the Walters Art Gallery; Mary Pauling Martin of the Star-Spangled-Banner Flag House Association; Mrs. Laura Brown of Langsdale Library of the University of Baltimore; Leroy B. Merriken, James A. Hartzell, James Bready and Joseph Simpson, all of the Baltimore *Sunpapers*; Jack and Beverly Wilgus, of the Maryland Institute and Joseph Cromwell of the Telephone Pioneers of America.

C.J.

CREDITS
Produced by Stanley L. Cahn
Editorial Supervision by Harold A. Williams
Research Assistance by Frederick Rasmussen
Designed by Mossman Art Studio
Dust Jacket by Stanley Mossman
Typography by Modern Linotypers, Inc.
Printed by Universal Lithographers, Inc.
Paper: Patina by S. D. Warren Paper Co.

A KEY TO CONTRIBUTORS

This list identifies sources and donors of print items and photography used in the text. Each graphic is identified by the following letter code:

(AAB) A. Aubrey Bodine
(AC) Author's collection
(BD) The Black & Decker Manufacturing Company
(BGE) The Baltimore Gas & Electric Company
(BI) Blaustein Industries, Inc.
(BMA) The Baltimore Museum of Art
(BNA) The Baltimore News American
(BORRM) The Baltimore & Ohio Railroad Museum
(BS) The Baltimore Sunpapers
(BSO) The Baltimore Symphony Orchestra
(CBMM) The Chesapeake Bay Maritime Museum
(CCC) Commercial Credit Corporation
(CCI) Charles Center—Inner Harbor Management
(CPM) The Chesapeake and Potomac Telephone Company of Maryland
(CS) Center Stage
(DP) Dover Publications, Inc.
(DS) Don Swann, Jr.
(EPFL) The Enoch Pratt Free Library
(FHA) The Star-Spangled-Banner Flag House Association
(HOT) The Harford Opera Theater
(JHH) The Johns Hopkins Hospital
(KM) Kevin D. Miles
(LBM) Leroy B. Merriken
(LC) The Library of Congress
(MC) McCormick & Company, Inc.
(MDT) The Maryland Department of Transportation
(MHS) The Maryland Historical Society
(ML) McKeldin Memorial Library, University of Maryland
(MNB) The Maryland National Bank
(MPA) The Maryland Port Administration
(MR) The Rev. Michael J. Roach
(MT) Morton Tadder
(MW) M. E. Warren
(NA) The United States Naval Academy
(NASA) The National Aeronautics and Space Administration
(PE) Peter Egeli
(PM) The Peale Museum
(RC) The Rouse Company
(SHSA) The Steamship Historical Society of America
(SI) The Smithsonian Institution
(TM) Mrs. Theodore Roosevelt McKeldin
(TP) T. Rowe Price Associates
(USF) The United States Fidelity and Guaranty Company
(VSL) The Virginia State Library
(WAG) The Walters Art Gallery
(WC) The Wilgus Collection
(WHO) William H. Ochs
(WS) The Washington Star
(WWP) Wide World Photos